Hors

MW01288730

Janice M. Ladendorf

Volume 1:
Spanish Horsemen and Horses in the New World

Drawings by Jo Mora and Candace Liddy.

Photograph courtesy of Windcross Conservancy: Spanish Mustang Preserve, Buffalo Gap, South Dakota.

Horses from History
Volume 1: Horsemen and Horses in the New World

Printed by CreateSpace.

Available from Amazon.com, CreateSpace.com, and other retail outlets.

Available on Kindle and other devices.

For Dave Lucio,

who asked me,

"Were there any Mexican Cowboys?"

Table of Contents

Book 3: Historic Fiction

Horses From History
Volume 1:
Spanish Horsemen and Horses in the New World

Book 1: Vaqueros and Vaqueras

Drawing courtesy of Jomoratrust.com.

The Remarkable Vaqueros
Chapter 1: European Heritage

When the Spanish came to the New World, the only domestic animals they found here were dogs and llamas. They brought horses, cattle, sheep, goats, and pigs first to the Caribbean Islands and then to Mexico. As they moved north from Mexico City, they found an ideal country for ranching and raising cattle, but had to train their best peons to be vaqueros. Translated into English, vaquero means cowman or buckaroo. When the Spanish expanded into southern Texas, Arizona, New Mexico, and California, they needed even more vaqueros to handle their expanding herds.

In the early 1800's, Americans began moving into Texas where they soon collided with Spanish ranching enterprises. A long-standing controversy exists over how much influence the Mexican vaqueros had on the emergence of the American cowboy. Some believe the Americans brought all the information, skills, and tools they needed with them. Others believe the first Texas cowboys learned everything they needed to know from the vaqueros. In my opinion, neither of these views is the correct one. Regardless of the discipline, profession, or craft, we all stand on the shoulders of those who have gone before. The vaqueros and cowboys had to have shared a heritage beginning with the domestication of cattle in Europe.

When were cattle domesticated?

In prehistoric times, Aurochs (Bos Primigenius) were a species of wild cattle who roamed over Europe, Asia, and North Africa. Their size varied from location to location. The biggest ones stood over six feet and weighed three thousand pounds. This species has been extinct since 1627. Shown on the next page is a drawing of what a real auroch might have looked like.

Many scientists believe the DNA of an extinct species can never be completely re-created, but various breeds of domestic cattle have been used to produce cattle who strongly resemble the ancient auroch. Like the original aurochs, the re-created ones are fast, agile, fierce, temperamental, and dangerous.

The re-creation of the auroch turned out to be both easier and much faster than the scientists had anticipated. Their discovery explains why Spanish cattle could revert so quickly and easily to the temperament of their ancestors, the prehistoric auroch. This change occurred in Spain around 700 AD when bull fighting on horseback began. In the New World, it began when the open ranges gave so many cattle the opportunity to turn feral.

Three bovine ecotypes or subspecies eventually appeared in widely separated area. The first one is the humpless taurine (Bos Taurus). Taurine cattle were first domesticated in the Tarus Mountains of southern Turkey. The second one is the humped zebu (Bos Indicus). Zebu cattle were first domesticated in Pakistan. Bos Africanus appeared at a later date and is thought to be a cross between taurine cattle and the aurochs who originally inhabited North Africa. The photograph on the next page shows a taurine bull and a zebu bull with a human standing between them. The zebu is obviously smaller than the taurine. The aurochs of that area could well have been smaller than the ones who inhabited Europe.

Farming and the domestication of animals began in the Neolithic Age. In that age, humans still used stone or wood to make their tools and weapons. For many centuries, scientists thought cattle had been domesticated between 6,000 and 4,000 BC, but recent archeological research has moved this date back to the beginning of this age in 10,500 BC. Nobody knows how humans managed to trap, control, and tame the ferocious Aurochs. It still is and may always remain a mystery, but the Paleolithic ancestors of these men had hunted mamonths, aurohs, and other large animals with spears. There is still no way to know if the individual domestication sites had used similar or different tools and techniques to tame the wild cattle in their area.

Cattle had always provided humans with meat and hides, but not with milk. When they were first domesticated, they immediately became a living, mobile source of stored food and hides. To protect themselves from these fierce and dangerous animals, humans probably ate or castrated the troublemakers. This form of selected breeding is a slow process and it would have had to have gone on for many generations to reduce the size and increase the docility of domesticated cattle. When it had succeeded, humans could have used cattle as pack animals.

Since Neolithic humans were afflicted with lactase intolerance, they could not digest milk. This problem still affects sixty-five percent of the world's population. The development of lactase persistence requires a genetic change that probably began somewhere between 5,000 and 4,000 BC. Dairying techniques soon spread from India to the Near East and North Africa. Humans not only began drinking and cooking with milk, they learned how to preserve it by making butter, cheese, and yogurt. By 4,000 BC, humans had also discovered wooden wheels, designed ox yokes, and put cattle to work as draft animals.

What Human Life Styles Evolved to Utilize Domesticated Cattle?

The innovations described above led to the gradual development of three distinctive life styles for managing and using cattle. Idealized summaries of each style are given below.

1) The farming life style

In the tenth century, the horse collar and harness came to Europe from China. Before this time, horses and mules could only be driven in chariots or used as pack animals. After this time, they could be used as draft animals, but not for plowing. The first plows also appeared in the tenth century. They were made of wood, but tipped with iron and only oxen were strong enough to pull them.

After this time, a typical farming family owned a few dairy cows and some kept as many as twelve. Since the cows had to be milked twice a day, they usually spent their nights in a barn or byre and their days in pasture. Unless the family owned fenced fields and pastures, their cattle had to be driven out to graze and watched to keep them from damaging crops. The pastures they used could be owned by a single family or shared by many families. Farmers believed herding was a low status job and they gave it to relatively low status individuals, such as adolescent males.

With a few exceptions, farmers castrated their male calves and used them as draft animals. These steers became oxen, but cows and bulls have also been used in harness. Farmers normally kept two or more castrated males for their own work and sold the others. Once oxen had accepted the yoke, they became valuable draught animals. If they worked hard every day, they probably needed barley to supplement their hay or grass rations.

Since dairy cattle had to be handled every day and oxen normally worked every day, the ideal animal was docile, tame, and well trained. When cattle grew too old or weak to produce milk or labor in the fields, they were slaughtered. The tough meat of such old cattle could best be utilized in stews or soups.

This life style had one major disadvantage. Farmers not only had to raise enough food for their families, they had to cure enough hay to feed their cattle in the winter. The longer and harder the winters, the more stored food their animals would need to survive until spring. As farming practices improved, they may also have begun storing grain as winter feed for their livestock. When the cast iron plow was invented in the eighteenth century, then horses could also be used for plowing. Since hard working horses need the quick energy provided by grain, this innovation probably encouraged farmers to store more grain as winter feed.

2) The nomadic life style.

Nomadism first developed as an alternative to farming. Nomadic cattle expect humans to defend them from predators and in return, they accept human leadership. Humans took over the roles played by the cows who led the herd from the front and the protective bulls who followed it. Unlike farmers, nomads have no fixed homes. They travel with their herds as they drive them from pasture to pasture. Migrations are often seasonal and may cover long distances. Nomadic tribes often fight over pastures and raid each other's herds. They also may be at odds with farmers. The history of Europe is full of stories about the mounted nomadic tribes who came out of the east and destroyed farms, cities, and whole civilizations.

What nomads herd and how they herd them varies with the location. On the steppes, cattle can be driven from horseback, but they need too much water to live in real deserts. In more settled areas, tamer cattle could be driven by humans on foot. The drovers used used goads, whips, and dogs to help them. Nomads ate many of their cattle and used their hides, but some tribes also utilized their milk, blood, or other byproducts. Like milk cows and oxen, their cattle had to be tame and reasonably docile.

Naturally there are many variations to the nomadic life style. For example, the Magyar people settled in Hungary in the tenth century. Since then, herds of horses, cattle, and sheep have roamed the Hungarian plains or pustza. Their herders do have permanent homes, but live and travel with their animals for most of the year. In the winter, they return to their homes where their charges can have protection from the weather and be fed stored hay or grain.

Like the Spanish fighting bulls, the Hungarian grey cattle are closely related to the Aurochs, but they are docile and tame and have been bred to produce excellent meat. For domestic cattle, they are large. The males may weigh up two thousand pounds or as much as two oxen. The females have more blue in their coats and may weight up to thirteen hundred pounds.

Their herders or gulyas use whips and dogs to help them drive their herds. To get them to the best markets, they had to be able to drive them on foot for over six hundred miles. The illustration on the next page shows the harmonious relationship between these men and their animals.

3) The ranching life style

The ranching life style was the last to emerge and is a compromise between the farming and nomadic life styles. Like farmers, ranchers have fixed homes and graze their cattle on land they own or lease. They may also have to provide winter feed for their animals. Like nomads, ranchers had to be able to protect their herds and drive them for long distances.

In Spain, cattle were first utilized in farming. During the Bronze Age, Spanish farmers developed a dun breed of docile milk cattle. Like most domestic breeds, this one was much smaller than the wild auroch. In Roman times, Spanish cattle were supposedly so fat they could produce buttermilk with no whey in it. Starting in 711 AD, the Moors conquered most of the Iberian penisula. They loved milk and brought their zebu cattle (bos tarus indicus) with them. They probably captured, killed, and ate most of the dun cattle, but they could have bred some to their milk cattle. Like most farmers, they slaughtered cattle only when they became too old or weak to give them milk or labor. When the Moors were forced to leave Spain in 1492, they took their zebu cattle with them.

During the re-conquest, central Spain turned into a battle ground where agriculture was destroyed and far too many domestic cattle killed. As a result, the Spanish turned to ranching and became the first ones to use this life style. Bull fighting preceded ranching, but is closely related to it. Our records of the various forms of this sport go back to classical times. It began in Spain just before the arrival of the Moors. While the Spanish fought them, they used bull fighting on horseback to prepare themselves for battle. They used no armor in these fights, but often wore partial or light armour into battle. Spain never used chain mail or plate armor as did the knights in England, France, and Germany. For their bullfights, they needed and bred powerful and aggressive bulls. These bulls throve best in natural surroundings on ranches. A modern herd of such bulls is shown below.

To survive these fights, they needed horses who were courageous enough to face the enraged bulls and handy enough to evade their charges. Fortunately, they had bred such horses for many centuries. After the Moors left Spain, rejoneo or bull fighting on horseback was stopped for over two hundred years because it was so dangerous. At this time, matadors began to fight bulls on foot. The Spanish think of bullfighting on horseback as a sport for gentleman and bullfighting on foot as an inferior sport for peons. Rejaneo continued in Portugal, but gradually evolved into a safer and more humane sport. It eventually revived in Spain and it still exists there and in Mexico.

According to author Andrew Rimas, after the Moors left the focus in cattle breeding in Spain turned from milk to meat. When Andalusia turned out to be perfect for ranching, the black and savage fighting bulls (bos taurus ibericus) were crossed on other breeds. The result was animals with a thick hide, atrocious temper, zest for reproduction, and tough meat. They also gave little milk, refused to accept the yoke, and could only be herded by men on horseback. These cattle are one of the breeds the Spanish shipped to the New World.

By the time Columbus discovered America, the Spanish had already had centuries of experience with running beef cattle on open ranges. They had bred cow sense into their handy horses and knew how to brand, roundup, and conduct long cattle drives. Since classical times, branding had been used in many places to identify the ownership of slaves and animals. The nomadic tribes well understood how to drive herds for long distances, but did not always use horses. Unlike these tribes, the Spanish always used horses and rarely used dogs. In the ranching style, the focus shifted away from staying with the herds to protecting the herds within the specific boundaries of the ranch. This change required the development of new social organizations and special skills, such as conducting roundups on the open range. The Spanish took what they had learned about ranching with them to the New World.

Conclusion:

Humans use cattle for meat, hides, tallow, milk, and labor. Meat, hides, and tallow can come from wild or domesticated cattle. Aurochs were first domesticated in 10,500 BC for this purpose. Beginning in 5,000 BC, a genetic change allowed humans to digest milk and they quickly developed dairying techniques. By 4,000 BC, castrated bulls could be yoked together to pull carts with wooden wheels. Three distinctive life styles appeared. They are the farming style, the nomadic life style, and the ranching life style.

Before the Moors invaded Spain, the farming style was the dominant one. The Spanish fought the Moors for almost eight hundred years. During that time, bull fighting on horseback was used as a training ground for battle. The Spanish fighting bulls are an ancient breed and inherited their fierce temperment for the auroch. They have also been bred for aggresiveness. During the Reconquest, the Spanish began to replace farming with ranching. After the Moors left Spain for good, the Spanish turned almost entirely to the production of meat animals.

By 1500 AD, cattle had been domesticated for twelve thousand years. In the New World, the Mexican vaqueros and the Texas cowboys began with far more knowledge than did those who first tamed the auroch. They inherited information, tools, and skills from their European ancestors.

Acknowledgements:

All photographs courtesy of Wikpedia.

The Remarkable Vaqueros
Chapter 2: English Colonies in the New World

By the time Europeans discovered the American continents, they had tamed, handled, herded, and bred cattle for thousands of years. Since the early explorers found no cattle in the Americas, each group of colonists had to bring both their cattle and their inherited skills with them. What breeds of cattle they brought varied from area to area. Each one was selected and bred to suit the desired life styles. From their first landings, the New England colonies followed the farming life style. The first colonists in the Carolinas also followed the farming style, but cattle raising eventually moved west towards the frontier and utilized the ranching style.

Who were the Puritan Cowboys?

Most of the Puritan colonists came from farming communities in England and intended to follow the same life style in the New World. Since the Devonshire cattle lived near the British ports; in 1623, the Puritans began by importing cattle from North Devon. This hardy breed of medium sized, multipurpose cattle was the ideal one for a farming life style.

Their milk is high in butterfat and can be turned into excellent cheese or butter. They produce high quality meat and make excellent draught animals. As a breed, they are active, intelligent, and strong, but cannot easily be handled by novice drivers. They are also easy to feed and fatten on a high forage diet.

As they settled in the New World, the Puritans established small towns surrounded by unfenced fields and common pasture lands. To keep their cattle out of the crops, they had to stalled at night. Early in the morning, a herdsmen drove them out to graze and at night he returned

18

them to their owners. This routine allowed for milking the cattle twice a day. The men who herded the cattle did not have a high status in the community. In 1647 a law was passed requiring all cattle and horses to be branded with two brands, one to identify the owner and one to identify his or her common pasture.

At that time, English farmers still used oxen as draught animals and regarded horses as mounts for noblemen. The Puritans soon discovered how useful horses could be as pack animals or riding horses. In the English winters, stock did well outside with some supplemental feeding. In New England, the colonists found winters to be far more severe. When their stocks of preserved food and hay ran low, the starving time began for both people and animals.

The Pynchon family found a way to resolve this problem. In 1635, William Pynchon founded the town of Springfield in the valley of the Connecticut River. He soon grew wealthy from the fur trade and his stock throve on the rich riverside pastures. In 1646, he discovered an excellent market for meat in the British owned islands of Barbados, Bermuda, and Jamaica. To better serve his customers, he built the first commercial American meat-packing plant.

His son, John, turned out to be just as innovative and interested in profit as his father. In 1654, he tried a new procedure. He imitated the Caribbean buccaneers or pirates when he fenced a small field, built a shelter, and fed his cattle all winter. Body heat keeps animals kept inside warm so they need far less to eat. Along with hay, his men gave his cattle vegetable scraps from the kitchens, malt-hops-barley residues from home brews, pulp from the cider mill, and similar protein supplements. By spring his cattle were plump, gentle, and friendly. His men drove them one hundred miles across the Old Bay Path to the Boston common where his fat cattle amazed the hungry colonists. Their sale yielded a good profit for their owner and others soon imitated him. This drive was the first recorded American trail drive.

Contractors soon began shipping Irish cattle to the New World. In Scotland and Ireland, herders drove their cattle for long distances, but they did not use horses, they used dogs to help them. Between 1640 and 1660, many of these men were shipped to the colonies and sold as indentured servants. They probably would have used familiar techniques on the trail drives. The only breed of horse ever developed in colonial New England was the Narragansett Pacer. These horses were used for riding and racing by the well off, but not for handling cattle by the low status drovers.

The Puritans probably did not use horses to handle their cattle. Branding and roping from the ground are techniques Europeans had used for thousands of years. They had also learned how to herd cattle on foot and horseback. Cattle who are regularly fed and handled by people can be safely be driven by humans on foot while cattle who have gone feral need to be driven by men on horseback.

Specialized breeding for meat or milk began in the early eighteenth century. From their initial imports, the New England farmers developed a uniquely American breed of Devon cattle. From New England, it gradually spread as far south as Florida. The picture below shows an example of the American Milking Devon at Mount Vernon.

How did Spanish Cattle reach the English Colonies?

On his second voyage to Florida, Ponce de Leon brought horses and cattle with him. When the survivors fled in 1521, their horses were so valuable they probably took them back to Cuba, but they may have left some cattle behind. When the Spanish returned, they brought more cattle with them and ranching in Florida soon became a profitable business. In their attempt to Christianize and civilize the Indians, Spanish missions and ranchos spread north as far as modern Charleston. As the Spanish colonists gradually retreated back to Florida, they left both horses and cattle behind for the English settlers. By 1706, there were no longer any Spanish people left in the lands claimed by English colonists in Virginia, the Carolinas, and Georgia.

Florida remained in Spanish hands until 1821. Within their borders, they could keep their strains of cattle and horses relatively pure. In the 1830's, many Americans began crossing Spanish cattle with other cattle breeds, but some stayed with the Spanish criollo breeds. Today the Florida Cracker cattle are small to medium sized, as well as docile and relatively easy to manage. They are hardy and known for their resistance to parasites. They produce excellent meat and resemble retinta cattle, one of the three breeds the Spanish brought to the New World. Unlike the Texas Longhorns, their horns grow up instead of out. Some believe maneuvering through the Florida brush selected for this shape. They are also called Cracker or scrub cows. They are shown in the photograph below.

How did Ranching Begin in South Carolina?

In 1670, English colonists began settling on the coastal lowlands of South Carolina. They imported their first stock from other colonies, but feral Spanish cattle and horses already roamed there. The Spanish had bred cattle mainly for meat. To get more flexibility, the southern colonists crossed them with multipurpose breeds, like the emerging American Milking Devon. Horse racing was popular, but initially limited to quarter mile races. The first racers were Spanish or Chickasaw horses. Unlike the Narragansett Pacers, these horses were quick, handy, and born with the cow sense needed for dealing with semi-feral cattle. They are one of the foundation stocks used to create the American Quarter Horse.

While the colonists were looking for a good cash crop, they followed the farming life style. They grazed their cattle on common pastures; but to keep them tame, the slaves brought them into pens every night and fed them something. In the winter, what they got was corn blades and crab grass hay. The colonists shipped meat to the Bahamas and Bermuda. These British owned islands were only a week's sail from Wilmington or Charleston. When rice turned out to be valuable as a cash crop, stock raising moved west to the Piedmont.

The first cow pen community was established on the frontier in 1710. It was near the fall lines of the Savannah and Pee Dee Rivers. They sold their meat, leather, and work animals to planters in the eastern low-country and to British owned islands in the Caribbean. Investors looked for the tall grass savannas where their cattle could graze on the luxurious cane and pea vine grass. They also wanted marshes nearby for winter grazing. Most of them owned the acres around the actual settlements, but not the pastures their animals grazed every month of the year. They followed the ranching life style.

A standard cow pen community had a house for the manager, cabins for the workers, gardens, land cleared for corn, and spacious pens for the animals. The pens had wings so herds of cattle, horses, and hogs could slowly be driven forward until they could be pushed through the open gate into the pen. From time to time, herds had to be driven into the pens for special tasks, such as branding, gelding, and sorting out cattle to be driven to the eastern markets. In the winter, many communities also fed cattle in the pens. Every cow pen community had its own unique brand. In the larger communities, cattle could be divided into herds who had their own pasture areas and pens. The pens were usually about ten miles apart. In this warm climate, animals needed a lot of salt. To keep the animals close to the pens and familiar with people, salt was regularly scattered outside of them.

Who were the Cow Hunters and Crackers?

The keepers or supervisors of the cow pen communities were usually white, as were some of the workers. As in New England, Scotch and Irish men were shipped to the southern colonies and sold as indentured servants. When they had served their time, they often settled on the frontier. Many German and Swiss immigrants moved south from Pennsylvania and joined them. The farther west the cow pen communities moved, the more white frontiersmen may have worked for them. When white workers disappeared, sometimes they turned into stock thieves or outlaws. The rest of the workers were black and mostly enslaved. Some of them fled to freedom with their horses.

By 1724, ads for slaves to work in the cow pen communities identified them as cow hunters. Many of them had initially come from areas in West Africa, such as Ghana or Gambia, where they had lived as nomadic herders of cattle. Their new owners soon discovered how many useful skills they had brought with them. Some even had experience in handling horses. These men soon figured out what jobs could best be done on horseback and which ones should still be done on foot. They may have been the ones who used salt to keep stock near the pens.

The cow hunters used also used a blacksnake whips. These whips had hardwood handles about three feet long and lashes ten to fifteen feet long. A special tip was used to give the whip a sharp, popping, or cracking sound. The men who used those whips often achieved a high degree of accuracy. As they drove cattle into towns, they liked to announce their arrival by cracking their whips and people began calling them crackers. In their early days in Texas, they did use these whips but soon found better ways of handling the ferocious longhorns there. Today they are still used in Australia where they could have been introduced by loyalists fleeing from the American Revolution.

The last technique involved the use of what they called bulldogs. These hounds drove cattle by nipping at their heels and held them by grabbing their noses with their teeth. Some of the breeds they used were Catahoulas, Tennessee Brindles, and Leopard Dogs. An innovative black cowboy imitated these dogs when he learned how to hold cattle motionless with his teeth. He is credited with starting the modern rodeo sport of bull dogging.

From South Carolina, the cow pen communities spread into North Carolina and Georgia. In the 1750's, pastures suffered from over grazing and an epidemic wiped out most of the cattle in this area. After the Revolution, the lands once used by the cow pen communities was gradually converted to cotton. Cattle raising moved west first to Kentucky and Tennessee where the land was forested and well watered. In the 1820's, they began moving to Texas where they found a whole new world of open plains, brush, and feral longhorn cattle. What they took with them was their Chickasaw horses and their bulldogging hounds.

Conclusion:

In New England, colonists used the English farming life style and their cattle began to starve in mid to late winter. The innovative John Pynchon introduced the idea of providing cattle with shelter and supplemental food during the winter. His trail drive to Boston in the spring yielded a fat profit and others began imitating him. Their tame and docile cattle could be driven on foot. These colonial farmers created a new breed, the American Milking Devon.

In the seventeenth century, the Spanish established missions and ranches in Florida, Georgia, and the Carolinas. When they pulled back to Florida, they left many horses and cattle behind. When the English settlers came, they found these animals. They caught, tamed, and bred them to stock imported from the other colonies.

The colonists in South Carolina soon found a lucrative market for meat in the British owned Caribbean islands. Their cow pen communities used the ranching style, but in heavily wooded areas. Many of the slaves imported from West Africa had been nomadic herders and they applied their skills when they were sent to these communities. To drive cattle, cow hunters and crackers used Chickasaw horses, blacksnake whips, and bulldogging hounds.

Acknowledgements:

All photographs courtesy of Wikipedia.

The Remarkable Vaqueros
Chapter 3:
Ranching with Vaqueros in Spain and Mexico

The Mexican vaqueros and the Texas cowboys shared a common heritage beginning with the domestication of cattle in Europe. Three distinctive life styles had evolved there - the farming style, the nomadic style, and the ranch style. The ranch style was first used in Spain and the Conquistadors brought it with them to the New World.

How did the ranching style evolve in Spain?

In the eleventh century AD, cattle ranching began in northern Spain in the provinces of Leon and Castile. As soon as the Spanish had taken Andalusia back from the Moors, they introduced cattle ranching there. The terrain in Spain is similar to much of what the Conquistadors found in New Spain. New Spain included what became Mexico, southern Texas, Arizona, New Mexico, and California. The photograph below is of Andalusia.

The Moors drank milk and ate many milk dishes. When they left Spain, they took their milk cattle with them. By that time, the Spanish no longer wanted to own and breed cattle for milk. They focused on breeding cattle for meat and the fighting arena. Instead of using docile oxen for draft work, they preferred to use mules. The

King of Spain gave George Washington the first mules to live in the United States.

As soon as the Spanish ranchers began running cattle on the open ranges, they had to brand them and use their handy, highly trained horses to herd them on their periodic roundups and overland cattle drives. As they bred more and more aggression into their range cattle, soon only men on horseback could safely approach them.

Protective Associations for Ranching

Well before 1500 AD, Spanish ranchers had discovered two types of systems that gave them good results. According to author Joe S. Graham, they imported both to the New World. They were the seigneurial and municipal systems.

During the long war with the Moors, large areas of land had been devastated and if they lacked population, ranchers simply moved their cattle into these lands and took control of them. Little or no attempt was made to regulate the seigneurial system of land grabbing. In New Spain, the same system was used by the missions as they established themselves on the unpopulated frontiers.

In municipal or private ranching many people owned a few cattle who usually grazed together on ranges around the town. To manage conflicts among the ranchers and farmers, municipalities developed the mesta or stockman's guild. It regulated grazing rights, compensation for crop damage, wages, branding, periodic roundups, removal of unbranded strays, marketing and slaughter, and penalties for breaking the rules. Problems with unbranded and stolen cattle start whenever cattle are run on open ranges. When they occurred in the New World, the Spanish introduced the mesta organization to resolve them.

The Vaqueros in Spain

The Spanish ranchers employed two types of vaqueros. They utilized both freemen and bonded servants. Freemen contracted for a year. At the end of each year, they were paid with cash or cattle or both. Some were permitted to run their cattle with the ranch herd. Bonded servants were tied to whoever had taken over their debts and they were not paid regularly.

The larger the herds, the more vaqueros would be needed to care for them. Crews always included a foreman or mayoral and could have three to twelve vaqueros. Some crews used dogs to help them herd cattle. The larger crews often included a "conocedor" who had to memorize cattle descriptions so he could identify strays or lost stock.

How did Ranching begin in Mexico?

Cattle first came to the New World in 1498. By the early 1500's, livestock raising had spread to Puerto Rico, Jamaica, Cuba, and other islands in the West Indies. Spanish cattle thrived on these islands and some escaped and turned feral. Most of the cattle sent to Florida and the southeastern missions were shipped out of Cuba. When the Spanish retreated to Florida, they left both cattle and horses behind in South Carolina and Georgia. To obtain cattle docile enough for draft work, the Carolina Crackers crossed feral Spanish cattle with stock imported from the other English colonies.

What the Spanish brought to the New World was three breeds of cattle - the barrenda (piebald), the retinto (tan or reddish), and the ganado prieto (the black Andalusian fighting bulls). They shipped them first to the Caribbean Islands, then to Florida, and finally to Mexico. They may never have brought any of the aggressive ganado prieto cattle into their southeastern settlements, but they certainly brought some to Mexico. As these three breeds adapted to their new environment, they mixed to create the Texas Longhorn. The photo below is of this famous breed.

The Conquistadors who came to Mexico were interested in gold and glory, not in establishing settlements or ranches. When the Aztecs drove them out of Tenochtitlan, the Conquistadors lost all the gold they had gathered. Some eventually settled down on land grants given to them by the Crown. Cortez owned twenty-two Indian settlements in the Valley of Oaxaca and registered the first cattle brand in New Spain (Mexico).

Gregoria de Villalobos imported the first cattle to Mexico. When he became the lieutenant governor of New Spain in 1521, he spent much of his time coordinating the arrival of settlers, supplies, and livestock. The area between Vera Cruz and Mexico City turned out to be ideal for cattle raising. When too many cattle were exported from the West Indies, the Islanders stopped the flow until too many people complained to the King.

Protective Associations

When ranchers began grazing their unbranded cattle on the lands south and west of Mexico City, they let them wander at will. Many destroyed Indian irrigation channels and crops. In return, the Indians slaughtered and ate some of their cattle. The Spanish answer to this explosive situations was to create a mesta (rancher's guild). At first, it dealt only with brand registration and stray or stolen animals. As ranching expanded, so did what the mesta controlled. The first mesta in New Spain became the prototype for stockmen's associations in both Mexico and our southwestern states.

Native Labor

To support and expand their new colony, the Spanish had to use native laborers. Their first workers were Aztec captives so they decided to try out the Aztec encomienda system. It required Indians to labor a set number of days each week as their chiefs or the Spanish gentry directed. This system rapidly became abusive. When religious organizations had filed enough complaints with the Crown, the government replaced it with the repartimento system. It allowed them to rent workers to the landowners, but it also failed. In both cases, the cause of the failures was the ninety-five percent decline in the native population. The deaths came from the European diseases the Spanish unknowingly brought with them.

At first, the Conquistadors did not allow Indians to ride horses, but somehow the Spanish landowners and mission priests had to find train, and keep enough vaqueros to handle the day to day care of their expanding herds. As the need for vaqueros steadily increased, this law was ignored and eventually canceled. For a short time, vaqueros could own their own horses and equipment, but in 1574, a new law forbade them to own horses or sell stock. This law was part of the restructuring that created the hacienda system. Some of the vaqueros turned into bandits (banditos), but most settled down to working for lower salaries on the new haciendas.

The final solution of those who ruled Mexico was the hacienda system. It was not used just in ranching, but in any profit producing enterprise of significant size. Many of the ranch owners or hacendados preferred to live in urban luxury and send their managers or estancios out to live on their landed estates or ranches. Their workers (peons) had job security, but were paid minimal wages plus basic housing, food supplies, medical care, and clothing. What they actually received probably varied with both time and place.

If the peons needed or wanted anything else, they had two choices. One, they could make it or grow it themselves. Two, they could buy items from the ranch store at prices set by the owners. Some stores sold quality items at reasonable prices while others did not. Most of the peons soon fell into debt and their children inherited their debts.

The hacienda system was designed to create bond servants. No one who owned the estate money could legally leave as long as he owned money to the estate. Debt peonage is not an unusual system and has been used in many forms through history. In the late nineteenth century, similar systems trapped workers in company towns and freed slaves into an exploitive system of share cropping and tenant farming.

Who were the vaqueros?

Ranch managers and friars from the missions selected some of their best peons to train as vaqueros. They had to be young, strong, and athletic. Most of the men who became vaqueros were mestizos, who had both Spanish and Indian ancestry; but some were Indians, descendants of Negro slaves, or mulattos with mixed Indian and Negro ancestry.

Many of the friars in the missions were sons of the nobility and had been taught fine horsemanship. They trained vaqueros in a series of steps. A student had to master each step before he could go on to the next phase. In the drawings on the next page, a friar is showing Mission Indians in California how to brand cattle. In the second drawing, he is giving a lesson in horsemanship.

Both drawings are by artist Jo Mora (see his biography under supplemental material).

Independent Cowboys and Superior Peons

The term, cowboy, was first used in Ireland about 1000 AD and by the New England drovers in the seventeenth century. During the American Revolution, the cattle thieves who sold meat to both sides called themselves cowboys. During the Mexican American war, cowboys rustled cattle from the Mexicans to feed the American troops. When the Americans first came to Texas, they called themselves vaqueros. About 1870, they begin calling themselves cowboys, cowpunchers, or wranglers.

Unlike the cowboys in the United States, the role played by the vaqueros in New Spain was not romanticized. They never became more than peons, but they were superior peons because they faced danger every day and used horses. They only did work if it could be done on horseback. They expected the inferior peons to do the type of manual labor cowboys often had to do. The working vaqueros could never expect to be promoted beyond the level of foreman (caporal).

The managers and owners (hacendados) may have practiced vaquero skills, but they thought of themselves charros. The vaquero badge of honor was the roweled spurs (espuelas) they wore with or without boots. The photograph below is of such spurs. The silver mounting would probably have been too expensive for a vaquero to purchase, but the hacendados and estancios could afford such embellishments to their equipment.

The vaqueros carried a long knife in a scabbard hung on their right leg. Unlike the cowboys, they never carried guns. They were too expensive for them to purchase and difficult to use from horseback. Our romantic image of a cowboy always shows him carrying a revolver in a holster at his side, but these guns were only good for killing humans and rattlesnakes at short distances. Rifles or carbines had to used for longer distances.

Cowboys and vaqueros may have done the same basic job, they led different lives. Vaquero means cowman. Most vaqueros were married and stayed on one hacienda all their life. They knew their animals and the land they grazed. As they grew older, their patron usually found them less strenuous jobs.

Cowboys were mostly young, single, and footloose. They rarely saw a woman. Some were lucky enough to find permanent jobs on well managed ranches, a few managed to start their own spreads, but many spent the time between trail drives or roundups without a job. Ranchers often described them as lazy, violent, immoral, or as low class drunken derelicts. Rancher's associations sometimes blacklisted unsatisfactory cowboys. Eventually most of the drifters got shot, hung, or found other occupations.

Conclusion:

Ranching began in Spain during the Reconquest. Two systems of ranching developed: the seigneurial (mission) one and the municipal (private) one. Stockmen's guilds or mestas emerged to manage conflicts between members of the municipalities who grazed their cattle on the open range. In Mexico, the Spanish tried the encomienda system, then repartimento system, and finally the hacienda system. To regulate the haciendas, they developed mestas similar to the ones in Spain.

The vaqueros were peons, but superior ones who rode horses and expected the inferior peons to do any manual labor. Unlike cowboys they were usually married men and stayed in one place. Most of the vaqueros were mestizos, but some were pure Indians. A few were descendants of Negro slaves or mulattos with mixed

Indian and Negro ancestry. The Spanish trained them, but held them in debt bondage for all their lives.

Spanish Vocabulary

banditos	bandits
barrenda	piebald cattle
caporal	foreman
conocedor	vaquero who specialized in brand recognition
encomienda	forced labor
espuelas	spurs
ganado prieto	black cattle, fighting bulls
mesta	stockmen's guild (association)
repartimento	rented labor
retinto	tan cattle
seigneurial	system for dividing large tracts of unoccupied land among owners

Acknowledgements:

The two drawings were done by Jo Mora (see his biography under supplemental material). They are used with the permission of the jomoratrust.com.

The first two photos are courtesy of Wikipedia.

Remarkable Vaqueros
Chapter 4: Vaquero Lifestyles

When the Conquistadors came to the New World, they brought the Spanish ranching style with them, but had to redesign it to suit the type of labor they found there. When they developed the hacienda system, the law allowed them to hold their peons in debt bondage.

How did the Vaqueros Live?

In English, ranch is the word used for all types of ranches. In Spanish, there are words to describe three types of ranches. Rancho is a small one worked by the owner. In the free period before the new law in 1574, some vaqueros earned or acquired cattle and started their own ranches. A hacienda is a medium sized ranch, normally found in central and south Mexico. It would have one headquarters for the owners and the ranch employees. Finally, the latifundio is a huge ranch divided into management areas and is found mostly in north Mexico. One of the American counterparts is the King Ranch.

Housing

In the early days, a ranch headquarters often was a fort. The owner and his family lived within its walls, but it would have space for a chapel, storerooms, workshops, stables, and the ranch store. The employees and their families typically lived in huts inside the walls. As the Indian and bandit threat declined in south Texas, the owners might live separately in a stone house, but one they could quickly turn into a fort. Their peon families lived in jacals, one room huts with dirt floors, whose standard size was ten by fourteen feet. The walls could be built out of mud (adobe), grass, or wood, but most of the roofs were made out of straw. In southern Texas, every one of them had a small alter (altarito).

Food and Hours

Although the hacendados provided families with their basic food supplies, the wife had to supplement it with purchases from the ranch store and what could be grown in her own small garden. She usually planted corn, beans, and pumpkin vines near her jacal. Most families had a few chickens, a goat, and maybe a pig. Their basic diet was meat, beans, rice, and camp bread. Cooking was mostly done outside and the family might eat their meals in ramada or shaded arbor. Good cooks produced delicious tortillas, tamales, and enchiladas. Over the years, Mexican food has become increasingly popular in the United States.

Unfortunately, vaqueros did not get to spend a lot of time with their families. They worked six days a week for twelve to fourteen hours a day. On their work days, the hacienda provided them with meals. Along with caring for their horses and equipment, their work schedule left them little time for recreation. Whenever their hands were free, they could braid rawhide and sometimes they sang while they worked.

During roundups they could be gone for days. Sometimes they spent weeks or months out on the range watching over the cattle. When they were far from home, they lived in crude lean-tos. They ate atole (corn meal mush), beef, and wild game. They also made a hot drink (pinole) with corn powder, cinnamon, and sometimes added chocolate.

What the vaqueros wore

Vaqueros clothing reflected both their dual heritage and what worked well for them in their jobs. The Indians knew how to weave natural fibers and they used that skill to create sombreros with wide brims to protect themselves from the sun. Others adapted European leather and felt hats to provide similar protection. They wore bandanas, shirts of cotton or wool, and short jackets (chaquetas). When it rained, they could wear waterproof leather jackets or ponchos. Their pants tied at the sides and went only to the knee. They wore no boots and often went barefoot. If they had shoes, they were made out of buckskin.

The Invention of Chaps

In northern Mexico and our southeastern states, they often had to ride through a country full of thorny acacia trees and plants, like cactus, who also produced thorns. Below the knee, they wore leather leggings (botas) to protect their legs. When they didn't provide enough protection, they tried hanging two huge slabs of rawhide (armas) from their belts. One fell on their right side and one on their left side. Later they used narrower slabs (armitas) and tied them together below the knee. These were the first chaps. They could be fringed and made out of buckskin, calfskin, or the pelts of goats, sheep, bear, wolf, or lion.

The drawing below by Jo Mora illustrates the great variety in what individual vaqueros actually wore. It shows three California Mission Indians.

How did the vaqueros play?

The vaqueros did not work all the time. Fiestas and rodeos were part of their life style. The smaller events could be just for those who lived on a ranch. On the California ranches, biweekly holidays occurred on the days when cattle were killed and meat handed out to vaquero families. Neighbors could be invited to share in larger fiestas. Whenever ranches held large scale roundups, rodeos would follow. Once a vaquero's belly was full, he liked to sing and could dance all night. The drawing below is by Jo Mora.

The bigger the gathering, the more competitive events would be included. Various types of races were common, as were gambling on the results. In match races, two horses competed against each other. Depending on the length of the race, horses could be tested for speed or for speed and endurance.

For a rayar race, a line would be drawn on the ground. Two horses started at a gallop from the same distance away, but they came from opposite directions. When the riders halted them, the one who stopped with his front feet closest to the ground line was the winner. This type of racing tested the rider's skill and the horse's training.

A ring race (la sortija) tested a vaqueros skills. Two posts about ten feet high would be set up and linked with a beam. A ring would be loosely suspended on the beam. The vaquero would have to race underneath it and catch the ring on a twig or pencil. Failures were common and bets would be placed on who would catch the ring. These races are still popular in Argentina and Chili.

Another common event, run at the rooster (carrera del gallo), is shown below in the drawing by Jo Mora. To succeed, the vaquero would have to catch the chicken's head and pull him out of the ground.

The vaqueros also had more dangerous contests. They were not content with just roping and riding bulls. A more difficult event was colear or tailing the bull. Using this method to throw a bull required strength, great skill and perfect timing. The drawing below by Jo Mora shows a California Mission Indian tailing a steer (coboda).

Another dangerous event was the ride of death (paso de la muerte). The vaquero had to gallop his horse close to a wild horse so that he leap across onto its back. He had to stick on this horse until he quit bucking or running. By the horse came to a halt, he had probably over come his fear and accepted his rider. The Mexican mustangers (mesteneros) used this method for catching individual wild horses.

Along with all the other contests, vaqueros enjoyed demonstrating their roping skills and their ability to stick on a bucking bronco. Ideally the vaqueros trained their working mounts so well they never learned to buck, but sometimes they enjoyed catching and breaking mustangs in a few days. A wild horse, who is fighting for his life, will typically buck.

The five main events in modern rodeos are riding bucking broncos with saddles, riding bucking broncos without saddles, riding bulls, calf roping, and bulldogging. The first four events derived from vaquero contests and the fifth was first done by a Negro cowboy. The drawing on the next page by Jo Mora shows a bucking bronco in action.

Straight up
and scratching.

Conclusion:

The vaqueros lived in huts (jacals) and their basic diet consisted of meat, beans, rice, and camp bread. They developed clothes suited to their job, such as sombreros, and invented chaps. They worked long hours, but enjoyed festivals where they held many types of contests, some of which turned into modern rodeo events. Whether these contests were or are harder on the men or the animals is impossible to determine.

Spanish Vocabulary

atole	corn meal mush
botas	leather leggings, knee to ankle
altarito	alter
chaquetas	short jackets

colear	tailing the bull
cobeda	tailing the steer
carrera del gallo	run at the rooster
hacienda	medium sized ranch with one headquarters for owners and staff
jacals	huts
la sortija	ring race
latifundio	hugh ranch with multiple management areas
mesteneros	mustangers
paso de la muerte	ride of death
pinole	hot drink with corn powder, cinnamon, and sometimes chocolate
ramada	shaded arbor
rancho	small ranch, worked by owner
rayar	race when two horses race towards straight line from opposite directions

Acknowledgements:

The five drawings were done by Jo Mora. They are used with the permission of the jomoratrust.com.

The Remarkable Vaqueros
Chapter 5
Vaqueros At Work - Saddle Design and Use

Ranching in New Spain (Mexico) placed new demands on the vaqueros. To do their job, they needed suitable horses and a new type of saddle.

What kind of horses did the Vaqueros Ride?

When Columbus discovered the New World in 1492, there was more than one breed of horse or pony living in Iberia. The Andalusian had been bred for war, hunting, and herding cattle. They were compact horses who were naturally balanced and exceptionally agile. For hundreds of years, the nobility had ridden these horses into battle or in confrontations with the fierce Spanish cattle.

The Sorraia was an ancient breed who many believe is the ancestor of the Andalusian. These two breeds were similar, but the Sorraia was smaller and tougher. What the Spanish vaqueros rode was probably mostly Sorraias. Both breeds were known for their cow sense and endurance. Iberia also had various pony breeds.

Since there were no horses in the New World, exports to the Caribbean began immediately. The small tough Sorraias had a better chance of surviving the arduous ocean journey than did the larger Andalusians. Beginning with the Cortez expedition, the Spanish started shipping horses from the Islands to New Spain (Mexico).

In Mexico, the Spanish owners (hacendados) and ranch managers naturally preferred to ride highly trained Andalusians. Before the implementation of the hacienda system, vaqueros could own their own horses, but all they could afford was the smaller Sorraias. What the vaqueros needed was tough, hardy, handy horses with great cow sense. They also had to be brave enough to face and handle the fierce Spanish cattle. Many documented instances exist of bulls deliberately attacking people on foot. Sometimes, they also attacked men on horseback.

To create the perfect cow horse, the hacendados began crossing their Andalusians with Sorraias. They probably rode the biggest and finest ones themselves, but the rest still served the vaqueros well. More information on these horses can be found in Part II.

The breeding programs established by these men was a great success. The drawing below by Jo Mora shows an early hacendado on a fine horse who came from one of these programs. His horse is wearing a breast collar, but not a martingale.

What Kind of Saddles did the Vaqueros Use?

In evaluating saddles, there are three critical factors. They must be comfortable for the horse to wear and never bruise or rub sores on his back. They must keep the rider safe, secure, and in balance with the horse. Finally, they must be designed to work efficiently for whatever type of the job the horse is asked to do.

Spanish Saddles

At the time of the Conquest, the Spanish used two types of saddles. Both were carefully fitted to insure the horse's comfort and keep the rider in balance with his horse. Both put the rider's weight right over the stirrups. The first was the Spanish war saddle (silla de mantura). It was heavy and cumbersome, but it wrapped around the rider and held him securely between the pommel and cantle. A drawing of one by Jo Mora is shown below. When the rider wore partial or light armor, he used this saddle and rode with longer stirrups.

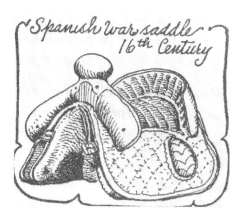

The second type of saddle was designed for the gineta style of riding (silla gineta) with shorter stirrups and more bend in the rider's knees. As compared to the war saddle, it had a lower fork and cantle, but did not yet have a horn. It was not as secure as the war saddle, but gave the rider more flexibility. Since the vaqueros often had to ride fast over rugged terrain, they needed flexibility so they used the gineta saddle.

While the war saddle was designed to keep the rider secure when he used long lance to kill his enemies, the gineta saddle was designed to let a rider use a shorter lance to kill animals and men. During the drought years, the California vaqueros used lances to kill wild horses, as is shown in the drawing below by Jo Mora. The vaquero is riding gineta style with shorter stirrups and a bent knee.

The same type of lance was an indispensable and decisive weapon for the cowboys (gauchos) of South America. They developed the ones they used from Indian spears, but modified them to be more vicious. Instead of a stone or wooden point, they attached the blade of a shearing scissors to the end. To make their lances, they used a long bamboo cane or a straight staff of hard wood. It took great courage to use one in battle and the men who did so were greatly admired.

Vaquero Saddles

According to author Frank Dean, the final design for the vaquero saddles (silla de vaqueros) had been created by 1750. They were the gineta saddle with a horn for dally roping and special rigging. When animals were

47

roped, extra strong rigging had to be used to hold the saddle on the horse. The cinch ran over or through the saddle tree. At first, these saddles had a narrow horn. Later, they changed to a larger, platter shaped horn. Initially, they used the Spanish rigging that fit underneath the horn. This type of saddle is shown in the drawing below by Jo Mora.

As time passed, several changes emerged. One was the addition of large, square skirts (bastos) to protect the legs of the rider. Another was the use of tapederos to protect the rider's feet. The drawing below by Jo Mora shows a saddle with both of these features.

Later, they developed a center fire rig where the single girth is in the middle of the saddle, but attached to both the pommel and the cantle. A Vaquero saddle is similar to the modern A-fork or slick fork saddle and is still used by those who practice vaquero horsemanship. Although Mexican vaqueros and Texas cowboys may have used the same saddle, the cowboy usually rode with longer stirrups. A drawing of a slick fork saddle by Jo Mora is shown below.

In Mexico, vaquero saddles may be called charro saddles and they are widely used in cowboy (charro) competitions. The first photograph below shows a charro standing on his horse and twirling his lariat. The second one is of charros riding in a parade. All are wearing traditional woven sombreros with wide rims.

Saddle Making and Covers

Hacendados expected their vaqueros to provide their own equipment. They used available materials to make their own saddles and tailored them to suit their personal horses and preferences. Their saddle trees and stirrups were made out of wood. Their girths were often made out mane hair taken from mares. If they had goats, their girths could also be woven out of mohair. To cover the saddle they used rawhide. Rawhide is cured, but not tanned.

Cured hides are stiff and must be softened to exactly the right degree before they can be used. The saddle was first covered with softened rawhide; then the covering was damped so it would tighten as it dried. The vaqueros also used rawhide to make their bridles, saddle accessories, and leather clothing.

Like the McClellan saddle, the vaquero saddles were not particularly comfortable for the riders. The vaqueros used mochillas to resolve this problem. They were rawhide covers cut to fit over the whole saddle. A saddle with a mochilla is shown in the drawing below by Jo Mora.

For fiestas or parades, a vaquero could also throw a fancy curaza over his the mochilla. For long rides, he could add a corona with pouches. To protect special items to the back of the saddle, he could also attach an anquerra or flanker to the back of his saddle. The Pony Express riders used mochillas to carry the mail. When they switched horses, all they had to do was throw the mochilla over the saddle on their new horse. The mochilla they used is shown on the next page. It combined features from the mochilla, the corona, and anquerra.

As time passed, charro equipment and clothing grew more elaborate. The drawing by Jo Mora on the next page shows a California hacendado in 1840 riding a highly trained horse.

Cowboy Saddles

When the Americans started moving into Texas, they learned from the vaqueros, used vaquero equipment, and

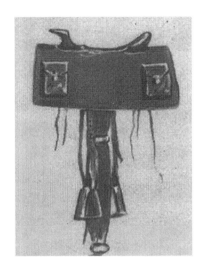

called themselves vaqueros. The word, cowboy, did not come into use until 1870. The first true western saddle appeared in 1850. The Mother Hubbard saddle is a vaquero saddle, but with the mochilla permanently attached to the saddle. It is still a center fire saddle. Like the one shown on the next page, it is covered with tanned leather instead of rawhide.

The Texas cowboys introduced the double rigging that utilized both a front and back cinch. An earlier version of this type of saddle is the first one shown in the drawing on the next page. A later version is shown in the third drawing. As soon as saddlers began using tanned leather, they could crave patterns into the leather. The center fire saddle in the middle of the drawing is such a saddle. Silver could also be used for decorations. All three drawings of these saddles are taken from one by Jo Mora.

Today handmade vaquero or charro show saddles are extremely expensive. Since modern vaqueros no longer make their own gear, their skill of working with rawhide has almost been lost. Working vaqueros now buy the same equipment as do cowboys and wear similar clothes.

Conclusion:

When the Spanish came to the New World, they brought their horses with them. Survival and their breeding programs produced an agile, fast, and courageous horse who could face, herd, and rope fierce cattle who towered over him. The vaquero saddle evolved from the Spanish war and gineta saddles. When the vaqueros added additional rigging and a horn, they could use their horses as a mobile snubbing posts. These were the first western saddles.

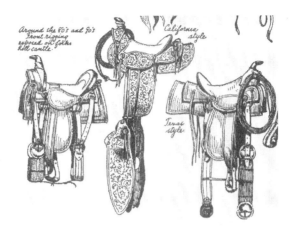

Spanish Vocabulary:

anquerra	flank cover behind saddle
bastos	saddle skirts
corona	cover for mochilla with pockets, used on trail before the development of saddle bags
curaza	fancy cover for mochilla often used at fiestas
gaucho	South American cowboy
gineta	style of riding with shorter stirrups and bent knees
hacendados	hacienda owners
mochilla	rawhide covers cut fit the whole saddle
rejoneo	bull fighting on horseback
silla de mantura	Spanish war saddle
silla de vaquero	vaquero saddle
silla gineta	saddle used for gineta style riding with shorter stirrups and bent knees

Acknowledgements:

Illustrations 1, 3-7, 10, 12, 14 drawings are by Jo Mora. They are used with the permission of the jomoratrust.com.

The photographs of charros and the mochilla are courtesy of Wikipedia.

The Remarkable Vaqueros
Chapter 6
Vaqueros at Work - Catching, Throwing, and Killing

Under the hacienda system, superior peons became vaqueros and to do their job, they needed new ways to catch, throw, and kill cattle. They tried many techniques before they discovered how to make lassos (lariats). This tool was the most effective when they used it with a saddle which had special rigging and a horn for roping.

New Challenges

When the Spanish brought their horses and cattle to Mexico, they encountered both familiar and unfamiliar environment conditions. They started haciendas in areas where there was little or no wood available to build corrals or pens. In these areas, they had to apply what they had learned in Spain to roundup their cattle without any enclosures. They also started haciendas in areas where thorny trees and plants thrived. Weaving through these areas to catch or drive cattle was a difficult task and required the development of new tools.

As settlements moved north, every day the cattle had to travel farther to find enough grazing. The ones who survived had endurance and a rangy build. Some of their ancestors had been bred for bullfighting and there are many documented incidents of these cattle attacking humans on foot and sometimes attacking humans on horseback.

In Spain, predators had always been hunted for sport and to protect domestic animals. In the New World, the natives had no reason to hunt similar species. Instead of being protected by men, range cattle had to learn to defend themselves against predators, such as wolves, mountain lions, grizzly bears, and poisonous snakes. The ones who survived were big and soon became fast, agile, and increasingly aggressive.

What did the Mexican vaqueros use to catch or throw cattle?

Experiment 1 - The Garrocha

What vaqueros still use in Spain to herd cattle is an iron tipped lance (garrocha). This tool was developed from the lances used in battle. In ranch work, they are used as cattle prods. A skilled vaquero can also use one to knock a bull, steer, or cow right off his or her feet. For both rider and horse, the skills needed to use a garrocha effectively take time to develop. Today garrochas are still used on Spanish ranches, in the sport of Doma Vaquera, and to control fighting bulls in the Mexican arenas. The photograph below shows a modern trainer carrying a garrocha. He is using a gineta saddle.

In New Spain, the vaqueros experimented with garrochas, but they can be awkward to carry and difficult to use in brush country. For their work, they had to find a better alternative.

Experiment 2 - The Hocking Knife

As cattle proliferated, they became valuable for their hides and tallow. New Spain shipped thousands of hides annually to Spain. Vaqueros soon began using a hocking knife (desjarretadera or media luna) to kill cattle. It consisted of a half-moon shaped blade, sharpened on the inner curve, and attached to a stout pole from ten to twelve feet long. An example of a hocking knife is shown below.

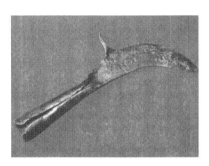

From horseback, the vaquero used his hocking knife to hamstring the selected animal. Once the cut had been cut, the helpless animal fell to the ground and could be paralyzed by striking it with the pole behind the knife. While the rider continued to cut more animals, others killed the cattle, skinned them, and removed the tallow. All too often, the meat would be left to rot. When this efficient method of killing began to decimate the herds, the mesta outlawed it, but it continued on the northern borders for years.

Experiment 3 - Nuqueo (Necking)

When a California rancher got a call for hides and tallow from a Yankee trading ship, he had to kill and skin the required number of cattle in a hurry. He selected them from his herds and his vaqueros cut them out and drove them over to the killing ground (mantanza). Two vaqueros could rope, throw, and hold animal for butchering, but there was a faster technique. A necker (nuquedore) could put his horse next to the animal and stab him at the nape of neck with a long knife. If the knife slid accurately between the right vertebra, it killed the animal immediately. This technique is called necking (nuqueo) and is shown in the drawing below by Jo Mora.

When the herd filled the killing pen, this technique was faster and more efficient than team roping. As the herd diminished, the cattle had enough space to run and dodge. While spectators enjoyed the thrilling chases, this technique became increasingly dangerous for both men and animals.

Experiment 4 - Limp Ropes

When the vaqueros could no longer use hocking knives, they tried adding a rope loop at the end of the similar type of pole. This technique had been used for centuries by the Mongols and Tartars. To be effective, the rider had to put his horse in a strategic position so the person or animal to be caught would be thrown off balance. It worked particularly well against mounted knights in armor. Like using the garrocha, this technique worked best in open country.

From the beginning of domestication, ropes had been used to trap and control cattle, but only from the ground. This technique worked best when the animal had already been herded into an enclosure, as the Carolina Crackers did. It was also used in Spain and taught to the Mexican vaqueros, but when the vaqueros tried roping from horseback, they encountered one major problem. Once they had the loop over the animal's head or horns, they had no way to anchor the rope to their horse. They tried hooking it to the cinch rings of their saddle and to the horse's tail or neck, but none of these techniques worked particularly well.

The Gauchos and Bolas (Boleadores)

Any of the cowboys in Latin America can be called gauchos, but this term is most often applied to those who herd cattle on the pampas of Argentina and Uruguay. Like the American cowboys, but unlike the Mexican vaqueros, these gauchos have been romanticized. The photograph below is of an Argentine gaucho, taken in 1968.

The gauchos from the pampas of South America shared their Spanish heritage with the Mexican vaqueros, but they drew more heavily on their Indian heritage. In Patagonia, the Indians used bolas (boleadoras) to capture game and birds. Just as the gauchos based their lances on Indian spears, they adapted Indian bolos (boleadoras) to the capture of running cattle. They also used them for hunting. The picture below is of a three ball boleadora.

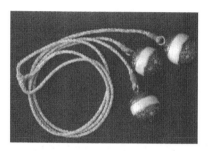

There are many types of bolos. Most of them use two or three balls. The design of the knot and cord varies, as does the weight of the balls. Gauchos use bolas with braided leather cords. Their balls could be made out of wood or sacks weighed with stones. The drawing below shows a gaucho hunting ostriches with a boleadora.

The gauchos rode gineta style with bent knees, but they had to design their saddles (recadoras) without using wood. Trees are rare on the pampas so the gauchos had to make their saddles out of leather and wool.

Who invented lassos (lariats)?

The development of vaquero roping required two inventions. First, vaqueros needed something to act as a mobile snubbing post. Some unknown vaqueros tried adding special rigging and a horn to their saddle. The other invention was the lasso or lariat. The vaqueros made their own lassos out of strips of twisted rawhide or fibers from the agave cactus. To give a lasso enough stiffness to hold a loop, they had wind the fibers around a core. They called the ones they made out of rawhide, reatas. On foot or horseback, they used it to loop and throw the rope to catch an animal. With cattle, they sometimes spun the rope before throwing it. The standard length for a lasso was thirty to sixty feet. Thirty feet worked best in brush country. In the open country of California, the vaqueros used longer lassos from sixty-five to one hundred and ten feet.

Lassos or lariats were used in two different types of roping. In dally roping, the lasso was wrapped around the horn, but not hard tied. The vaqueros designed their center fire saddles for this type of roping. In dally roping, as the animal started to fall, the lasso could be released. This technique minimized the shock to the animal and put less strain on the saddle. After the Civil War, the Texans introduced double rigging so they could actually tie the lariat to the saddle horn. Hard tying the lariat increased the jolt both to the animal and the saddle rigging.

Lasso can be used as a noun or verb. The verb came from the Spanish word, lazo, and the noun from an Americanization of reata. Lasso initially meant the limp ropes used by the vaqueros before they invented the true lasso with a core. Lariat initially meant the ordinary ropes used to picket horses. Today both words mean the special ropes used by charros, vaqueros, and cowboys to catch animals. According to author David Dary, lasso is typically used in California and lariat in the southwest.

The charros and vaqueros spent many years inventing and testing a variety of specialized loops and throws. The houlihan throw was what worked the best with horses. They enjoyed using their skills to catch any animal who moved, including coyotes, wolves, bears, prairie dogs, and eagles. To do trick roping, they spun their lassos. Their techniques made quite an impression on the Americans who came to Texas and they let vaqueros teach them their skills. The drawing below by Jo Mora shows California vaqueros roping wild horses.

What worked the best for the vaqueros on the King Ranch was dally roping in the brush and tying fast on the open range. By the end of the nineteenth century, horses had gotten bigger and cattle smaller. The most temperamental and obstinate bulls had also been eliminated. Unlike the Mexicans, the Americans also castrated most of the male cattle. These changes meant roping did not need to be as sophisticated, but the special loops, spins, and throws developed by the vaqueros are living on in charro performances.

After the Mexican Revolution early in the 20th century, the modern charro competitions (charreada) began. Nine of its events are limited to men. They are scored on points and judged on both style and execution. Only amateurs compete and they cannot receive any prize money. Some events, such as bull riding and bareback bronc riding, are similar to ones in our rodeos, but others are unique to Mexico. They include events featuring charro roping, tailing the steer (coleadero), and the pass of death (paso de la muerte). In recent years, a tenth event (escaramza) has been added for women. Teams of women ride their horses sidesaddle as they go through precisely choreographed patterns. This event honors the women of the revolution (adelitas).

Conclusion:

When the vaqueros added a horn and special rigging to their gineta saddle, they could use their horses as a mobile snubbing posts. These were the first western saddles. The vaqueros also invented lassos or lariats and they used them to throw a loop over the horns or around the feet of the animal they wanted to catch. The modern art of charro roping is based on the loops and throws they developed. This art includes using spinning ropes in demonstrations of trick roping.

Spanish Vocabulary

adelitas	women of the revolution
boleadora	bola
charreada	modern charro competitions
coleadero	tailing the bull by wrapping his tail around the rider's leg
desjarretadera	hocking knife or media luna - used to cut hamstrings in hind legs of cattle to be killed
escaramza	the one women's event in charro competitions
garrocha	iron tipped lance used to herd cattle
gaucho	cowboy from Argentina or Uruguay
gineta	style of riding with shorter stirrups and bent knees
lazo	lasso
mantanza	killing ground
nuqueo	necking - killing cattle with a knife

	inserted at the nape of the neck
nuquedore	a necker
paso del muerte	ride of death - leaping onto the back of a wild horse from another horse and staying on him until he stops bucking or running
recadora	gaucho saddle
reata	lariat

Acknowledgements:

The third and seventh illustrations are drawings by Jo Mora. They are used with the permission of the jomoratrust.com.

The photographs of the gaucho and boleadora are courtesy of Wikipedia.

The Remarkable Vaqueros
Chapter 7: Vaquero Horsemanship

Along with western saddles and lariats or lassos, the vaqueros also invented the bosal hackamore. It was a new type of bitless bridle and all of the foundation training in vaquero horsemanship was done with it. Some horses never got beyond this point. In more advanced training, the horse was first ridden with a bit and bosal, then with just some form of curb bit. Advanced training and riding was not an art mastered by every vaquero.

Spanish Horses and Horsemanship

Many fine horses came with the Spanish to the New Work. For thousands of years, these horses had been bred for war, hunting, and handling cattle. During the Moorish occupation, the art of fighting bulls on horseback emerged. For all these tasks, the horses needed to be quick, agile, spirited, and responsive to their riders. By the sixteenth century, horsemanship had become a fine art in Iberia. They believed a well reined horse should be able to execute all of the maneuvers we see today in reining and high school dressage. They also expected such a horse to have a soft mouth and to respond to feather light aids. Their goals and standards came with them to New Spain (Mexico). In vaquero horsemanship, a real expert could link his reins together with one single horse hair. To cue his horse, he could use one finger, but without breaking the hair.

What is a Bosal Hackamore?

The use of bitless bridles began with the domestication of the horse and may have preceded the use of bits. By the 5th century BC, the Persians had begun using a hakma, a thick plaited noseband to guide and collect their horses. In Spain, a cavesson with a stiff noseband was used with a bitted bridle in the horse's initial training.

In northern Mexico, the vaqueros developed their own form of jaqumia or hackamore. A handmade hackamore is shown below. It has four parts: the cabezada, the bozal, the fiador, and the mecate. In English, cabezada becomes headstall, bozal turns into bosal, fiador is corrupted to Theodore and mecate to McCarty. The bosal is the noseband, the mecate the reins, and fiador the keeper or safety latch.

The bosal is what really makes this type of hackamore unique. In all other forms of horsemanship, some form of contact through the reins is used to teach the horse to carry his head in the correct position. In a properly designed and fitted hackamore, the nose button and the heel knot are balanced so the horse can only make himself comfortable if his head is in the correct position. He will discover this position only if he is ridden on a loose or slack rein. A bosal must be firm, but flexible and have life or spring to it. Before he cues his horse, the rider begins by slightly lifting the bosal. This action warns the horse to expect a cue. Cues are similar to the light touches used in riding a sensitive horse with a bit. After the rider releases his touch, then the hackamore must spring back into the normal position.

To create this spring, the bosal must be made out of strands of braided rawhide wrapped around a rawhide core. The art of rawhide braiding began in Tibet, was borrowed by the Arabs, and brought to Spain by the Moors. Rawhide must be cured, but cannot be tanned or it turns into leather. To make a hackamore, only top quality hides should be used and they must be properly cured. When the bosal is made, the strands used on the outside must be tightly braided, the ends well tied, and strands beveled so they have no rough edges. This rule applies to the heel button and the sides of the bosal. Any edges may irritate, sore, or even cut the horse. In the photographs below, the first one shows a smoothly braided bosal and the second one shows a roughly braided bosal.

The photograph on the next page is of my Spanish Mustang wearing his hackamore. The bosal sits correctly on his nose where the bone ends and cartilage begins. This spot is thin skinned and extremely sensitive. This photograph was deliberately taken from an angle to show the gap between the horse's jaw and the heel knot. Again, this is a sensitive spot because only thin skin covers the horse's jaws. If the heel knot is too close to the jaws, the hackamore cannot work properly and may create sores underneath the horse's jaw.

67

In the photograph above, the bosal is used with a normal headstall and throatlatch. The handmade hackamore shown earlier uses no metal and is adjusted with ties. Another type has metal buckles and does not have a fiador. The fiador is used to hold the bosal in place so that it cannot slide down or off the horse's nose. If the hackamore does not have a fiador, it should never be used to lead or tie a horse. With a fiador, if the horse pulls back, the hackamore should stay on his head. In the first photograph below, the horse is pulling back and putting pressure on the fiador. In the second one, the horse is ready to follow his trainer and has put no pressure on the fiador.

The vaqueros typically lived on large ranches with no ready access to cities or stores. They had to learn how to make and clean their own equipment from the materials on hand. A mecate included reins and a lead rope. The material the vaqueros used for creating a mecate was hair taken the manes of mares or young horses. It was never taken from working horses. Tail hair from horses or steers was thought to be too stiff. The natural colors of the mane hair were often woven together to create attractive patterns. Mecates have also been made from cotton or mohair, but these materials may be too stiff for a sensitive horse. To keep his equipment functioning, a vaquero had to keep it clean. Unlike leather, rawhide must never be oiled, but it can be cleaned with homemade soap. During roundups, to protect his hackamore from dirt and sweat, a vaquero often greased it with mutton or beef tallow.

To be effective, a hackamore must be adjusted to fit the individual horse's head and temperament. Horses vary in sensitivity and docility. Choices and adjustments can be made to suit each individual. Stage of training is also a factor. The bosals used with colts are normally be heavier than the ones used with highly trained horses. The hackamore shown on a Spanish Mustang on the prior page is a heavy colt bosal. The photograph below shows a hackamore correctly fitted to a horse with a small muzzle.

How did the Vaqueros Produce Well Reined Horses?

According to author Luis B. Ortega, the old vaqueros who taught him always thought of their horses first. They saw them as individuals, studied their good and bad points, learned their peculiar characteristics, and never rushed their training. The old vaqueros let each horse learn at whatever speed suited him best. They might spend three to six months starting an unbroken colt and take years to turn selected individuals into well reined horses. Every step of the way, they used cattle to train their horses.

In those days, horses were not started until they were old enough to stay sound under the heavy demands of range work. The vaqueros did not ride mares. Colts were gelded and branded and then turned back out on the range until they were five or six years old. Domadors specialized in breaking horses who had run free on the range for years. They started every potro or unbroken horse with a hackamore. The drawing below by Jo Mora shows a colt being ridden in a bosal. The rider is holding the reins in one hand in the correct position for vaquero horsemanship.

When the colt was ready, the trainer put a bit in his mouth. When the horse had figured out how to comfortably carry the bit, they rode him with double reins. The hackamore reins were used to explain bit cues to him and, if necessary, to correct him. The drawing below by Jo Mora shows a colt being ridden with double reins.

What the domador was expected to produce was a horse who was easy to handle and safe to ride. When he

71

discarded the hackamore, the horse could usually be ridden in a normal bridle. Depending on the softness or hardness of the horse's mouth, his permanent bit could be one of many different types of curbs. If the domador felt he was best ridden in a bosal, the horse would not qualify for advanced training, but he could still become an adequate cowpony, like the one shown on the next page in the drawing by Jo Mora.

The men who handled advanced training were called arrendadors. They used one unusual training technique. They well understood the importance of cueing in rhythm with the right phase in the horse's gait. To help themselves, they liked to train early in the morning when they could watch the horse's shadow to see the position of his feet. They also applied this knowledge to roping. By watching the animal's feet, they could determine when to throw the rope so as to avoid injuring him.

Both they and the domadors had a wealth of knowledge about techniques they could use for dealing with specific types of horses or ones with special problems. Most of the domadors were young men while the arrendadors were older men with more years of experience. They selected the best horses for advanced training. Their job was to turn the horses they selected into well reined ones. Along with sensitivity to the bit, they also taught him to respond to the rattle of a spur touching the stirrup. They could take the horse away before from the domador before he had introduced him to the bit or wait until he had completed his initial training. If an arrendador did not select the horse for advanced training, he could be put to work either in a hackamore or some type of curb bit. Once they had learned their job, many became excellent cowponies.

The progression from a bitless bridle, to double reins, to riding with a bit is not unique to vaquero horsemanship. Some classical masters also followed this procedure, but they used cavessons instead of hackamores. This technique often avoids many of the problems that come forcing a horse to accept contact with a bit.

Another unique feature of vaquero horsemanship is the special bit they developed for exhibiting their finished horses. Like the jaqumia, spade bits are designed to work effectively on a loose rein and balanced so the horse has to carry his head in the correct position to make himself comfortable. Spade bits are the most misunderstood and abused bits in the world. They are signal bits and should **never** be used to hold any form of continuous contact with the horse's mouth. They are designed to be used with light pressure and can easily be abused by a rider who applies too much pressure or hangs on the horses mouth. Since they required so much sensitivity from both horse and rider horse, they are not the best bits to use when the team is working with cattle.

Change:

When the Americans started moving into Texas, they had to have been impressed with vaquero horsemanship. They soon learned the tools and techniques used by the vaqueros, but did not necessarily accept the goals and attitudes behind them. One of the vaquero goals was to have a horse who never bucked from his first to his last day of training. Ground work helped them achieve this goal. The cowboys soon adapted what they had learned from the vaqueros to achieve increased efficiency.

A domador or arrendador normally had a secure job and could afford to take however much time he needed to produce a well schooled horse. The Americans paid a domador a small sum, such as $2.50, for every horse he started. This procedure meant he could only afford to take one month to finish the job and could spend little time on ground work. When American bronco busters took over this job, the time shrank even more. According to author John Richard Young, cowboys preferred to ride half broke horses who still bucked and frequently tried to bite, strike, or kick their riders.

As the years passed, vaquero horsemanship gradually faded away in the United States. In the early twentieth century, only a few old vaqueros were left and they passed on their knowledge to a few interested men like Luis B. Ortega. By then, skilled trainers not only had to start colts, they had to attempt to reform horses who had been ruined by the rough handling of the cowboys who had been riding them. Instead of disappearing, today vaquero horsemanship has made a comeback with horsemen who want to ride their highly schooled horses in the same style as the old time vaqueros.

Conclusion:

The Spanish brought fine horses and fine horsemanship with them to the New World. The vaqueros invented the bosal hackamore and the spade bit. These tools are not designed to work on contact. The horse must be ridden on a loose rein and cued with feather light touches. The cowboys borrowed these tools; but in their search for efficiency, they often used them to break and abuse horses. They did not want to take the time needed to achieve the high degree of responsiveness desired by the vaqueros.

Spanish Vocabulary

arrendador	one who trains reined horses
bozal	bosal - noseband for jaqumia
cabezada	headstall for a jaqumia
domador	one who breaks horses
fiador	theodore - keeper or safety latch for a jaqumia
jaqumia	hackamore
mecate	McCarty - reins for jaqumia
potro	unbroken horse

Acknowledgements:

The last three drawings are by Jo Mora used with the permission of the jomoratrust.com.

The Remarkable Vaqueros
Chapter 8: Conclusion

All domestic cattle are descended from the auroch. Compared to modern cattle, aurochs were large, agile, fierce, and dangerous. By 10,000 BC, Neolithic man had begun the process of taming them. They used cattle for meat, tallow, and hides. Humans soon began selecting cattle for more docility and smaller sizes. Four or five thousand years were needed to breed cattle who could be used for dairying and draft work. When the Spanish came to the New World, they brought three breeds of cattle with them. One was the Iberian fighting bull. This ancient breed had inherited the fierce temperament of the auroch and had been bred for aggressiveness.

The tools and techniques for handling cattle depend on two factors. One is their intended use. The farming, nomadic, and ranching life styles have different requirements. Farming needs tame, docile cows who can be milked every day and castrated bulls who can be used for draft work. Nomads use cattle for meat, milk, and other products. As they migrate, they must be able to drive their herds with them. Ranching focuses on meat animals who may graze on large pastures or open range and have little contact with humans.

Regardless of the discipline, profession, or craft, we all stand on the shoulders of those who have gone before. Since cattle had been so long domesticated, the Mexican vaqueros and the American cowboys could draw on what their European ancestors had learned about handling cattle. For many centuries, Europeans had known about breeding, branding, castrating, roping from the ground, and driving herds of cattle for short or long distances.

The second factor is the physical environment. The New England Puritans had to learn to provide shelter and feed to their animals in their severe winters. The Carolina Crackers had unlimited timber available to build homes and pens for their animals. When they moved on to what would become Texas; they brought their Chickasaw horses and bull dogging hounds with them. Their Chickasaw horses came from the same Spanish bloodlines as did the Mexican cowponies. In Texas, they encountered both the southern brush country and open ranges where timber was hard to find. To deal with these new environments, they had to borrow tools and techniques from the Mexican vaqueros.

As a result of the Moorish conquest, ranching began in Spain and followed the Conquistadors to the New World. In northern Mexico and southern Texas, they found land similar to what they had utilized in Spain. As their ranching enterprises grew, they soon organized mestas like the Spanish ones. Ranching in Mexico was based on the hacienda system and selected peons were trained to be vaqueros. They invented sombreros, chaps, the center fire saddle, lassos (lariats), dally roping, and bosal hackamores. They enjoyed demonstrating their skills in contests at their fiestas.

In the early 1800's, Americans began moving into Texas where they collided with Mexican haciendas. In our southern states, they had used the ranching style to raise beef cattle, but in heavily wooden areas. In Texas, they encountered a new type of cattle. To survive, the Mexican cattle had turned into the ferocious longhorns. Those who handled them faced the same challenges as those who had tamed the auroch. This breed of cattle was large, tough, and extremely dangerous. They used their long horns like lances to attack each other, humans, and predators. They attacked humans on foot and even men on horseback were not entirely safe from them. The drawing on the next page by Jo Mora shows a feisty ladino sinking one horn into the belly of the vaquero's horse. The vaqueros accepted these dangers, but the cowboys soon began killing off the more aggressive bulls.

The Americans soon adopted the tools used by the vaqueros and learned how to use them, but they did not begin calling themselves cowboys until about 1870. Cowboy culture modified some of the vaquero traditions. The vaqueros only did work on horseback so they had plenty of time to spend training their horses. Cowboys had to do manual labor on foot so they had to get their horses ready to work much sooner. Instead of rawhide, the cowboys used leather to cover their saddles. To hard tie their lariats, they invented double rigging. As the horses got bigger and the cattle smaller and less hostile, less skill was needed to handle them.

To this day, ranching and cowboy vocabulary shows the influence of many Spanish words. Some words, like adobe, bandana, corral, hombre, loco, poncho, and tamale, came right over to English. When English pronunciation was applied to some Spanish words, they turned into new words. For example, vaquero turned into buckaroo and fiador turned into theodore. Other words, like cavy, dally, chaps, and mustang derive from Spanish words. A list of such terms is in the supplemental material.

The day of the working vaquero is almost gone, but his skills are still used competitively in both Mexico and the United States. Charro fashions have stayed relatively stable while cowboys fashions came and went in techniques, tools, and clothes. The drawing below by Jo Mora shows what happened when angora chaps went the limit.

When angoras went the limit.

Spanish Vocabulary

| ladino | Angry bull, steer, or cow |
| mesta | ranchers organizations |

Acknowledgements:

The two drawings by Jo Mora are used with the permission of the jomoratrust.com.

Spanish Horsemen and Horses in the New World

As I researched and wrote these articles, Wes Thomsen provided invaluable assistance. He not only loaned me books, he answered endless questions. Wes grew up on a ranch in Idaho and has both practiced and studied vaquero horsemanship. He and his wife, Jane Greenwood raise fine Spanish Mustangs. They helped me find, tame, and train my own Spanish Mustang. They are both part of his story, as told in *A Marvelous Mustang.*

I also wish to thank Peter Hiller for giving me permission to use some of Jo Mora's delightful drawings to illustrate my articles.

Supplemental Material

Summary of Contributions:

When Americans began moving into Texas, they soon collided with Spanish ranching enterprises. A long standing controversy exists over how much influence the Mexican vaqueros had on the emergence of the American cowboy. Some believe the Americans brought all the skills and tools they needed with them. Others believe the first Texas cowboys learned everything they needed to know from the vaqueros. The historical facts do not support either view. The list below includes every contributor to the evolution of the ranch style and western horsemanship.

European Civilization
    Catching and Killing
    Herding
    Breeding
    Castrating
    Branding
    Hauling with ox yokes
    Milking
    Roping from the ground with limp ropes
    Driving herds for short or long distances

Spanish
    Ranch style (cattle on open ranges)
    Mestas (ranchers' organization)
    Fine horses with cow sense

Mexican Rulers (Spanish)
    Hacienda System
    Modern charro competitions

Mexican Vaqueros
    Sombreros

Chaps
Rodeo Events
Vaquero (Center fire) saddles
Ropes that could spin (lassos)
Dally roping from horseback
Roping from the ground with lassos
Bosal hackamores

American cowboys
Bulldogging hounds
Leather covering for saddles
Double rigged saddles
Hard tied roping (lariats)

Humans depend on the discoveries and knowledge of those who have lived before them. The vaqueros and cowboys shared a heritage beginning with the domestication of cattle in Europe. When the Spanish brought cattle to the New World, their vaqueros had over three hundred years to develop their tools and skills before the Americans reached Texas. Their invention of the vaquero saddle and lassos were crucial discoveries in the evolution of western horsemanship. The first American cowboys learned from them and later added refinements to improve their tools and skills.

Joseph Jacinto Mora
A Short Biography

Jo Mora was a talented artist who lived a life full of adventure. As a young man, he acquired the skills of a working cowboy or vaquero. He was born in Uruguay in 1876, but his family moved to the United States a year later. He grew up in New Jersey and Boston. His father told him many stories about the South American gauchos. He gave his son an excellent education, but the lure of the Old West was too much for him. After a conflict with his publisher in 1903, he abandoned a promising career as an illustrator and cartoonist. He went west and never again lived on the East Coast.

When he took a job on John Donahue's ranch in California, he encountered several middle aged California vaqueros whose skills impressed him. They introduced him to vaquero horsemanship. Since he was fluent in Spanish, they enjoyed teaching him and telling him stories of their life and ancestors. In his book, *Californios: The Saga of the Hard-Riding Vaqueros, America's First Cowboys,* he states the vaqueros gave the original American cowboy the skills and equipment he needed to handle Spanish cattle on the Southwestern ranges.

After Jo discovered the camera, he spent three years with the Hopi Indians. His photographs of their lives are the Smithsonian collections. Wherever he went, he kept notes and drawings in diary. He described some of his adventures in his book, *Trail Dust and Saddle Leather.* This book is also a compendium of information about the life style, skills, and tools of the American cowboy. The many drawings in this book and *Californios* breath reality.

He applied his talents and knowledge to many forms of art. He produced drawings, paintings, sculptures, murals, animated maps, and historically accurate dioramas. In 1907, he married Grace Alma Needham, the daughter of a pioneer family. He was devoted to his family, but especially close to his son, Joseph Needham Mora. He often wrote notes and letters to his family illustrated with cartoons and sketches. The legendary family hero, a brave rabbit, stars in his first children's story, *Budgee Budgee Cottontail*. He died in 1949, just three weeks after he finished *Californios*.

English/Spanish Vocabulary

adobe	adobe
bandana	bandana
bosal	bozal (noseband of hackamore)
bosalillo	bozalillo (noseband)
bronco	broncho (untrained horse)
buckaroo	vaquero
caporal	caporal (foreman)
cart	carretas
cavy	caballada (herd of working horses)
chaps	chaparreras
cinch	cincha
concho	concho (bridle decorations)
corral	corral
dally	dar la vuelta (make the turn or turn around) dalle vuelta (dally roping)
enchiladas	enchiladas
fiesta	festival
frijoles	frijoles
hackamore	jaquima
hocking knife	media luna (des jarrretada)
hombre	hombre
jerky	charqui or carne seca
lariat	reata (braided rawhide rope)
lasso	lazo
latigo	latigo
loco	loco
majordomo	mayordomo (steward for owner)
McCarty	mecate (reins and lead rope for hackamore)
mota	tassel (decorations)
mustang	mesteno (also wild unbranded cattle)
mustangers	mesteneros
poncho	poncho
quirt	romal (noisemaker at end of hackamore reins)

ranch	rancho (small, managed by owner)
rancher	ranchero
remuda	remuda (herd of working horses)
rodeo	rodear (round up)
sombrero	sombrero
stampede	estampida
tamales	tamale
tapederas	tapederas (fancy stirrup hoods)
tapederos	tapederos (stirrup hoods)
theodore	fiador (keeper or safety latch for hackamore)
vamoose	vamus
wrangler	caballerango (horse wrangler, from Spanish for groom)

Information Resources

Chapter 1:

Carlson, Laurie M. Cattle: An Informal Social History. Chicago, Ivan R. Dee, 2001.
"History of Cattle Domestication",
 archaeloogy.about.com/od/domestications/qt/cattle.htm
"History of Cow's Milk from the Ancient World to the Present",
 milk.procon.org/view.timeline.php?timelineID=000018.
"History of Oxen", my.execpc.com/D4/6D/hiebj_rm/page3.html.
Jankovich, Miklos. They Rode Into Europe. London, George G. Harrap & Co., Ltd, 1971.
Ladendorf, Janice. "Invisible Vaqueros, pt. 1, Valley Equestrian News, Nov. 2014, pp. 8-9, 12.
Rimas, Andrew. Beef. William Morrow, 2008.
Vernam, Glenn R., "Stockmen Through the Years", Man on Horseback, Harper & Row, 1964, pp. 104-112.

Chapter 2:

Carlson, Laurie M. "Cattle Culture Comes to American", Cattle: An Informal Social History. Chicago, Ivan R. Dee, 2001, pp. 63-82.
Dobie, J. Frank. The Longhorns. University of Texas Press, 1980.
Dunbar, Gary S., "Colonial Carolina Cowpens", Agricultural History, vol. 35, @3, July, 1961, pp. 125-131.
Earle, Alice Morse. "Narragansett Pacers", New England Magazine, March 1890, pp. 39-42.
Howard, Robert West. "The Puritan Cowboys" and "Quarter Milers and Crackers", The Horse in America, Chicago, Follet Publishing Co., 1965, pp. 31-44, 55-63.
Ladendorf, Janice. "A Lost Breed: The Chickasaw Horse", Valley Equestrian News, July 2014, pp. 8-9.
Ladendorf, Janice. "Invisible Vaqueros, pt. 2, Valley Equestrian News, Dec. 1014, pp. 8, 14-15.
Otto, John Solomon. "Livestock Raising in Early South Carolina, 1670 to 1700: Prelude to the Rice Plantation Economy", Agricultural History, vol. 61, #4, 1987, pp. 13-24.

Chapter 3:

Dary, David. Cowboy Culture: A Saga of Five Centuries. NY, Alfred A. Knopf, 1981.
Freedman, Russell. In the Days of the Vaqueros: America's First Cowboys. NY, Clarion Books, 2001.

Graham, Joe S. "The Ranch: A Spanish Institution", pp. 9-10, "The Ranch in Mexico", pp. 11-17. El Rancho in South Texas. University of North Texas Press, 1994.
Ladendorf, Janice. "Invisible Vaqueros, pt. 3, Valley Equestrian News, Jan. 2015, pp. 8-9, 12.
Mora, Jo. Californios: The Saga of the Hard Riding Vaqueros. NY, Doubleday & Co., 1949.

Chapter 4:

Dobie, Frank J. The Mustangs. University of Texas Press, 1984.
Freedman, Russell. In the Days of the Vaqueros: America's First Cowboys. NY, Clarion Books, 2001.
Graham, Joe S. "The Ranch: A Spanish Institution", pp. 9-10, "The Ranch in Mexico", pp. 11-17. El Rancho in South Texas. University of North Texas Press, 1994.
Ladendorf, Janice. "Invisible Vaqueros, pt. 3, Valley Equestrian News, Jan. 2015, pp. 8-9, 12.
Mora, Jo. Californios: The Saga of the Hard Riding Vaqueros. NY, Doubleday & Co., 1949.
Monday, Jane Clements. Voices from the Wild Horse Desert: The Vaquero Families of the King and Kennedy Ranches. Austin, University of Texas Press, 1997.
Rojas, Arnold R. These were the Vaqueros. Alamar Media, 2010.

Chapter 5:

Beatie, Russel H. Saddles. University of Oklahoma, 1981.
Capurro, Enrique Castells. Gauchos, 1965.
Dary, David. Cowboy Culture: A Saga of Five Centuries. NY, Alfred A. Knopt, 1981.
Dobie, J. Frank. The Longhorns. University of Texas Press, 1980.
Graham, Joe S. "The Ranch in Mexico", El Rancho in South Texas, University of North Texas Press, 1994, pp. 11-17.
Ladendorf, Janice. "Invisible Vaqueros, pt. 4", Valley Equestrian News, Feb. 2015, pp. 8-9, 12.
Mora, Jo. Californios: The Saga of the Hard Riding Vaqueros. NY, Doubleday & Co., 1949.
Mora, Jo. Trail Dust and Saddle Leather. University of Nebraska, 1946.

Chapter 6:

Capurro, Enrique Castells. Gauchos, 1965.
Dary, David. Cowboy Culture: A Saga of Five Centuries. NY, Alfred A. Knopt, 1981.

Dean, Frank and Rodriguez, Dr. Nacho. Charro Roping. Wild West Arts Club, 2003.
Dobie, J. Frank. The Longhorns. University of Texas Press, 1980.
Graham, Joe S. "The Ranch in Mexico", El Rancho in South Texas, University of North Texas Press, 1994, pp. 11-17.
Ladendorf, Janice. "Invisible Vaqueros, pt. 4, Valley Equestrian News, Feb. 2015, pp. 8-9, 12.
Mora, Jo. Californios: The Saga of the Hard Riding Vaqueros. NY, Doubleday & Co., 1949.
Mora, Jo. Trail Dust and Saddle Leather. University of Nebraska, 1946.

Chapter 7:

Bridges, Mike. "Vaquero-Style Bridle Bits: What they are and how they work." Western Horseman, July 1998, pp. 32-37.
Dodson, Ruth. "Texas-Mexican Horse Breaking", Dobie, J. Frank, editor, Mustangs and Cow Horses, Texas Folklore Society, 1981, pp. 269-290.
Ladendorf, Janice. "Contact", Human Views and Equine Behavior, 2013, pp. 194-205.
Ladendorf, Janice. "Invisible Vaqueros, pt. 5, Valley Equestrian News, March 2015, pp. 8-9, 12.
Lea, Tom. The Hands of Cantu. Little, Brown, and Company, 1964, pp. 38-53.
Ortega, Luis B. California Hackamore. Sacramento, CA, News Publishing Co., 1948.
Young, John Richard. "Modern Horse-Training versus the 'Good Old Days' and Ways", The Schooling of the Western Horse, University of Oklahoma, 1954, pp. 3-23.

Chapter 8:

Ladendorf, Janice, "Invisible Vaqueros, pt. 6, Valley Equestrian News, April, 2015, pp. 8-9.
Mitchell, Stephen. Jo Mora, Renaissance Man of the West. Ketchum, Idaho, Stoecklein Publishing, 1994.

The First Vaquera

A ghost rider haunts the prairies near Floresville, Texas. Many people have seen her riding over the hills near the San Antonio River on a white stallion with her long black hair flowing out behind her.

Who is this ghost? In life, her name was Donna Maria Del Carmen Calvillo and she lived from July 9, 1765 to Jan. 15, 1856. Where does she ride? Her ghost haunts her family ranch, the Rancho de Las Cabras (Ranch of the Goats). Why has her spirit returned to it? An analysis of her life could reveal the answer to this question.

In Donna Maria's day, married women in the United States could not legally own property, but in Spanish territory, women could inherit land and retain title in their own names. Sixty even obtained land grants directly from the Crown. Under these laws, Dona Maria could and did inherit the family ranch from her father. Under her expert management, it thrived under the rule of Spain, Mexico, Texas, and the United States.

In 1810, the census identified thirty surveyed ranches north of the Rio Grande River. Women owned and ran six of them. Although Donna Maria's father was still alive, the Ranch of the Goats showed as one of the six run by women. How did Donna Maria become one of these six women? Like all pioneer women, she had to be tough and strong to survive. Heredity, education, and experience all worked together to form her indomitable character.

Her intrepid grandfather came from the Canary Islands and settled in the wild country near the San Antonio River. He sold cattle and goats to the Mission San Francisco de la Espada. At that time, this Mission was on the northern edge of the Spanish settlements.

A report by a Franciscan priest named Juan Morfi suggested that many cattle might have been stolen from the Mission. In seven years, the Mission had lost over thirty thousand cattle, but not just to Indian raids. The neighboring ranchers had conduced many illegal roundups to brand strays from the Mission herds. He believed the Mission had become unprofitable in this perilous land.

When the Mission closed down, Dona Maria's father began a long battle to obtain title to some of the Mission land. In 1773, he claimed he had been given grazing rights by Padre Juan Botellos, the Superior of the Mission. Based on his years of possession, he filed a petition for a land grant with the Spanish government. In 1791, he was given title to the land he had used for so long on the northern part of the Mission's land.

In savage land, pioneering ranchers had to be prepared to defend themselves from Indians and bandits. Donna Maria lived in a fortress with three-foot walls and bastions for sentries. Living space for twenty families existed within these walls. Some had small rooms inside the house. Others built huts out of straw or mud within the fortress walls. Everyone who lived on the Ranch used their small chapel.

Dona Maria was the eldest of six children and her father treated her like a son. From childhood, he taught her to manage their land. Whenever she rode out with him, she wore men's clothes and rode astride in a man's saddle. Her actions shocked their neighbors. She worked beside her father's vaqueros or cowboys and soon proved she could outride, out rope, and outshoot any man. Her actions shocked their neighbors. They began calling her the first Vaquera. Since she had been born before our

Revolutionary War, she may well be the first American cowgirl.

As she grew older, many men came to court her. She could weld feminine weapons as skillfully as she could ropes and guns. She used her beauty to attract men and her charm to conceal her prickly tongue and naturally aggressive personality.

When she married Gavino Delgado, she kept her own name. Their two children died in infancy. When her husband began speaking out against Spanish rule, she decided she could not afford to alienate the authorities and risk losing her land. She denounced him and sent him away from her beloved ranch. Later, he was declared a rebel against the Crown.

With her father's support behind her, she could afford to flout convention. After she drove her husband away, she took many lovers to help her run the ranch. She had two illegitimate children, one by Juan Duran and another by a physician named Gortari. Despite the claims of her furious relatives, she formally adopted only one child - a young Indian boy. All through her life, she ignored the territorial gossip about her unconventional exploits.

In 1814, Indians killed Dona Maria's father. They had been led by her nephew, Ignacio Casanova. He was brought to trial for this murder, but there is no record of what happened to him. Since Dona Maria had become the head of the family when she inherited the Rancho de Las Cabras, she could have killed him or had him killed him to preserve their honor.

During the long war with Spain, she stayed neutral to protect her land and provided sanctuary to families and soldiers from both sides. After the war, she followed her father's example and spent fourteen years fighting to obtain legal title to her land from the new government of Mexico.

When she first approached the authorities, she wore a black dress and pretended to be a helpless widow. She claimed Indians or Spanish soldiers had stolen her title deeds. When playing feeble woman didn't work, she spent six years preparing a new survey of her land. She submitted it with a legal petition and finally won her long battle. By 1828, the government granted her title to two square leagues of land and in 1833, they acknowledged her ownership of an additional league. The total came to over 13,000 acres.

Under her management, the Ranch of the Goats supported up to twenty-five hundred cattle, nine hundred goats, and two hundred other animals. It served as a center for organizing cattle drives south to Coahuila. With the help of nearby families, Donna Maria built an extensive irrigation system, a granary, and a sugar mill.

When a large band of Indians encircled her home, she rode out to meet them with a gun in each hand and flying a white flag of peace. She cried, "Take whatever stock you want, but leave us in peace." They took twenty cattle, ate one, and drove the rest away.

After that, she paid tribute to all of the local Indian tribes. She always gave them food and occasionally included bullets and gunpowder with her gifts. Much to her neighbors' chagrin, the Indians never attacked her home again.

During the Texas Revolution, again she stayed neutral to protect her land and gave shelter to refugees from both sides. She always did whatever she had to do to keep faith with her land. She gave her life and love to it.

When she died, she left her property to another emancipated woman, her natural daughter, Maria Gortari. In death, maybe her indomitable spirit could not let go of her beloved ranch. Afterwards, it was sold, subdivided, and eventually abandoned. This outrage may have been final factor to bring her spirit back to ride over her land.

In 1995, the remaining acres became a historic site. Now that her ranch and her reign have received public recognition, perhaps her restless spirit may find peace at last.

Information Resources:

Moynihan, Dee Jacques, "Dona Maria, Rancher of Las Cabras", Texas Highways, August, 2002, pp. 26-29.

Acknowledgements:

Drawings courtesy of Candace Liddy.

Prior Versions Published As

"The First Vaquera", Apples N'Oats, Winter 2010, p. 55.
"The Phantom Vaquera", Valley Equestrian News, Oct. 2014, p. 12

Horses from History
Volume 1
Spanish Horsemen and Horses in the New World

Book 2: Iberian Horses:
From the New World to the Old World and Back
Again

Photograph courtesy of Windcross Conservancy:
Spanish Mustang Preserve, Buffalo Gap, South
Dakota.

Spanish Horses
Chapter 9: Equine Evolution

Introduction

The common ancestor of the horse, donkey, and zebra roamed the prairies of North America four million years ago. Horses evolved from that extinct species and their population has expanded and declined more than once. The latest episodes occurred 200,000 years ago and 25,000 years ago. Two to three million years ago, true horses began migrating to the Old World over the Bering Strait land bridge that once linked the continents. Many migrations back and forth are thought to have occurred.

Man and horse have co-existed for at least two million years, mainly in Eurasia. Our first relationship with them was one of predator and prey. Horses today may still carry memories of this time in their bodies, buried beneath the instincts that shape much of their behavior. Wild horses instinctively fear humans, just as they do cougars or wolves. These fears can still surface unexpectedly and explosively in domestic horses. One trigger may be our scent. Those who eat meat always give off a scent horses can quickly identify.

Between 13,000 and 11,000 years ago horses disappeared from their birthplace in North America. Controversy still exists over when and why this happened. The equine species may have died out more than once and been restored by migrations from Eurasia. Disease is one explanation for their final disappearance. Another is prehistoric man hunted them to extinction. Neither explanation accounts for the simultaneous disappearance of other large herbivores and the predators who lived off them. A changing climate may be the best explanation for the disappearance of all these species.

Like all other breeds of horses, the ancestors of the Spanish horse came from the prairies of North America. When the Conquistadors brought their horses with them to the New World, they returned to their original home. Are our mustangs feral or native horses? They are domesticated horses who escaped from man; but if their species is native to this continent, then they would have more protection under our current laws. Even though DNA analysis has determined they are native to this continent, this information has been rejected both by ranchers and those who make the laws governing the treatment of wild horses. Considerable controversy exists over whether or not a few members of the original species of wild horse survived and inter-bred with the horses brought over by the Spanish conquistadors.

As horses migrated from North America through Asia and Europe, they had to have encountered many variations in climate, elevation, and food supply. As equines adapted to these variations, they would have evolved into different types of animals. Environment does have considerable impact on body type. When the sun never set on the British empire, they discovered how much environment could influence equine body type. For example, when the British army imported horses to India, their descendants soon came to resemble the native animals who had already adapted to that environment.

True Wild Horses

Experts have identified four species of the true wild horse, each one of which evolved in a different environment.

a) The heavy forest horse (Equus Caballus Silvaticus)

This species thrived in the forested swamps of northern Europe during glacial times and has long been extinct. It probably evolved into Equus Caballus Germanicus. Traces of a heavy bodied, slow moving horse have been found in Scandinavia and dated at 12,000 BC. Other traces have been found in northwest Germany and dated at 3000 BC. They are believed to be the ancestors of our modern cob and draft breeds.

b) Przewalski's horse (Equus Caballus Przewalski).

About 50,000 years ago, this species split off from equus caballus and survived in eastern Asia until recent times. When bred to true horses; in two generations, the offspring no longer has the two additional genes of Prewalski's horses. A few members of this species were preserved in zoos and some of them have been returned to the wild in Mongolia. Below are two photographs of Prewalski's horses.

Is there any genetic relationship between Przewalski's horse and the Mongolian pony? Due to its intractable temperament, some believe it could not have been the anccstor of any of our modern breeds, but it did run on the same open ranges as the Mongolian ponies. Some recent research suggests there is no relationship, but one could have been created by stallions stealing domestic mares. The Mongolian pony is thought to be the ancestor of various other Asian breeds. As it migrated west with invading tribes, it may also be the unacknowledged ancestor of various European breeds.

c) The tundra horse

This species may have once lived in Siberia, but according to author Elwyn Hartley Edwards, sightings of herds of wild white horses were reported northwestern Siberia as recently as 1964. It is probably one of the remote ancestors of the Yakut pony. This breed can survive in Polar climates because it has short, wide feet and an exceptionally heavy coat. Some traces of similar DNA have recently been found in the wild herds of Chilcotin in British Columbia. The Yakut pony is shown in the photograph below.

d) The tarpan (Equus Caballus Gmelini)

This species ranged over Eastern Europe and Western Russia. The tarpan is thought to be one of the main ancestors of our modern breeds of light horses. The last true member of this species was killed in the late 19th century. The photograph on the next page was taken in 1884 and alleged to be of a tarpan, but some think it is a half-bred or feral horse.

In 1841, a artist named Borisov did draw a live Tarpan yearling who had not yet had time to grow a full mane or tail. This drawing is shown below. In my opinion, it does resemble the photograph above of the alleged Tarpan.

Three efforts have been made to re-create the Tarpan by breeding back from domestic breeds. The first one is the Konik horse, bred back from farm horses that are native to Poland. Tarpans once roamed this area and are thought to have been ancestors of these horses. They are now recognized as a normal equine breed.

The second one is the Heck horse, bred back from the Konik, Prewalski's horse, Gotland ponies, and Icelandic ponies. Gotland ponies come from a remote island in Sweden and are thought to be direct descendants of the tarpan. Although these horses have been marketed as

101

tarpans, scientists do not regard them as true members of this extinct species.

The third is the Hegardt or Stroebel horse, bred back by an American rancher from mustangs and ranch horses. They do resemble the Konik and Heck horses, but appear to be more compact and refined. In my opinion, they are more like Sorraias, a Portuguese breed that strongly resembles the tarpan. Some believe this is another species of the true wild horse and the ancestor of the Andalusian.

Below first there are two photographs of the Konik horse, and then there are two photographs of the Heck horse.

The Konik Horse

The Heck Horse

In my opinion, the first true horses were probably stocky, compact, and heavy boned with relatively short backs. Horses with this build need less fodder and can quickly spin around and kick to defend themselves. Depending on early nutrition, their size could have varied from thirteen to fifteen hands. Their color was probably bay. In the late 1800's, an American cavalry officer traveled round the world looking at all kinds of horses. He believed feral horses tended to revert to this type of steppe pony, as they have on Sable Island east of Nova Scotia.

Climate does affect equine body type. Horses, who endure cold winters and have to dig through the snow for their food, need to be heavier than those who live in warmer climates. Horses, who live in areas with mild winters and hot summers, need to be more refined. When the tarpan pony migrated south into the arid regions of Central Asia, a new type of horse may have evolved. It was a taller, lighter, and more refined horse. It was probably influenced both by environmental adaptation and selective breeding by humans. This breed had been established by 2,000 BC and was known as the Turkemenia or Turkoman horse. A drawing of it, done in 1848, is shown below.

Domestication

Feral horses have ranges and will defend their core territory against intruders, but they have shown true territorial behavior only when they are trapped within relatively small areas. Their evolutionary history demonstrates they are willing to travel in search of better pastures and more safety from predators.

When humans domesticated them, two new factors entered into their lives. They could be subjected to selected breeding and forced to migrate with their owners.

Breeding for human goals probably did not begin until relatively late in the domestication process. Evolution encourages the survival of the fittest, but human desires may work against this process. For example, breeding for lighter bone may increase beauty, but make the horse more prone to lameness.

Considerable controversy exists over when and where horses were first domesticated. Unlike other animals, horses showed no obvious physiological changes from domestication. For example, when wolves turned into dogs, they lost their long noses. An archeologist cannot look at an equine skeleton and determine if it was a wild or domestic horse. He must use other archaeological evidence and prepare to have its validity questioned by other scientists.

On the grasslands of the Ukraine, southwest Russia, and west Kazakhstan, extensive research has established horses were probably domesticated there sometime between 6,000 and 4,000 B.C. Some experts argue domestication spread all through Eurasia from this one site; but if it had, we'd all be drinking kumiss or fermented mare's milk. Also, modern DNA research does not support this hypothesis. It has established an incredible diversity in the mare lines of most of our modern breeds. A special analysis of ancient Chinese horses found all seven of the haplogroups identified in modern horse breeds.

In my opinion, if domestication had come from one center; then tack used by these early horseman would have been much more standardized. For example, the vaqueros of Mexico and the gauchos of Argentine started from the same source, but are far apart geographically. The vaqueros developed western saddles and lassos (lariats) while the gauchos used treeless saddles and boleadors.

Archeological evidence also suggests other sites did exist. Iberia is one of them. Domestication had probably occurred there between 6,000 and 4,000 BC though some experts believe horses were domesticated there well before this time. By 2,000 BC, the Andalusian had been established as a breed. When Arabia was not yet a desert, the Al-Magar civilization thrived near northern Yemen. Some of the artifacts from this site suggest horses may have been domesticated by 6,000 BC.

Various attempts have been made to link modern breeds to types of wild horses. The standard classification is of two pony types and two horse types. Authors tend to claim different breeds are descended from these types. Other classifications of three to seven types also exist. In my opinion, those who invented these classifications overlooked the extent to which human migrations have redistributed equine populations. War and commerce explain most of them. For example, horses were redistributed all through the Roman Empire. Starting about 200 B.C., the silk roads linked China to the Mediterranean and for centuries horses moved along these roads. The prime example of human induced migrations is what happened when the Conquistadors brought horses back to North America and introduced them to South America.

Conclusion:

When horses evolved on the prairies of North America, a land bridge often linked Alaska and Siberia. They used this bridge to migrate to Eurasia where they found many variations in climate, elevation, and food supply. As they adapted to these variations, four basic types of wild horses emerged. They are the heavy forest horse, Przewalski's horse, the tundra horse, and the tarpan. Only Przewalski's horse is not extinct. Three attempts to recreate the tarpan have been made. They are the Konik, the Heck horse, and the Hegardt or Stroebel horse.

About 12,000 BC, the horse disappeared from North America, but so did other large herbivores and the predators who preyed on them. Explanations vary from disease to over hunting by humans, but the most likely explanation is some type of climate change.

Horses were probably first domesticated between 6,000 and 4,000 BC. Extensive research has established this had happened on the grasslands of the Ukraine, southwest Russian, and Kazakhstan. Arid Turkmenistan lies south of Kazakhstan and by 2,000 BC, a special breed of horse had been established in this area. Other domestication sites do exist, such as Iberia. By 2,000 BC, the Iberian breed had been established there.

Domestic horses no longer had the freedom to migrate with their own herds, but they traveled far with their owners. When the Silk Roads ran from China to the Near East, they could spread along this road from east to west and from west to east. When the Conquistadors brought horses with them to the New World, where they once again returned to their original home.

Acknowledgements:

All photographs courtesy of Wikipedia.

Iberian Horses
Chapter 10: Prehistoric Heritage

On the equine migrations from North America to Eurasia, the Iberian Peninsula is one of the farthest points reached by the wild herds. Except for its northeast border with France, Iberia is surrounded by water. The Atlantic Ocean lies to the west and north and the Mediterranean Sea to the south and east. In the northeast, the Pyrenees form a barrier between it and the rest of the European Continent. Despite the distance and these barriers, horses did get there.

Cave paintings in the Iberian Peninsula go back to 30,000 BC and they show two general types of horses who have coexisted for thousands of years. The first type inhabited the north while the second type thrived on the fertile lands in the south. Both types eventually evolved into the various Iberian breeds. When Columbus discovered the New World, these breeds already existed.

The Garrano, Galician, and Asturian

The first type is well represented in the Iberian cave paintings. It began with the Garrano and came to include the Spanish Galician and Asturian. Most experts believe these breeds derived from horses who drifted south to escape from the ever expanding glaciers. When the Conquistadors took a few of them to New World, they traveled even farther.

The Garrano is the pony shown in these cave paintings. It may have a dished face with a round eye and is thought to be the remote ancestor of both the Spanish Galician and Asturian. The modern home of the Garranos is in northern Portugal and they are mostly used as a pack ponies, especially in mountainous areas. They are hardy, tough, and surefooted, but do not have a docile temperament. In recent times, an attempt has been made to improve this ancient breed by introducing some Arab blood into it. A photograph of a Garrano is shown below.

The home of the Asturian is on the northwestern coast of Spain. In classical times, these amblers were known as Asturcones and greatly valued for their easy gaits. In medieval times they were called haubvini in France, palfreys in England, and hobbies in Ireland. The ancient kingdom of Asturia, including Galicia, was never conquered by the Moors. A photograph of an Asturian is shown below.

The Galician is now almost extinct, but its original home was in the far northwest corner of the Iberian coast. When the semi feral herds were rounded up every fall, some were turned loose, but others kept to be put to work or compete in trotting races. A photograph of a Galician is shown on the next page.

Along with the Garrano, the Galician is thought to be the ancestor of the Mexican Galiceno. This cross produced small horses who are hardy, brave, gentle, intelligent, easy to train, and have great stamina. Since they are easy gaited and have a natural running walk, the Asturian was probably also one of their ancestors. Two photographs of a Galiceno stallion from the Suwannee Horse Ranch are shown below.

Modern DNA analysis has shown breeds from northern Iberia are closely related to the British pony breeds, especially the Exmoor. When the Celts migrated across Eurasia, they took their fine horses with them, some of whom were gaited. On their travels, they left many gaited breeds behind them. When settled in northern Iberia, most experts believe they bred their stallions to native mares to produce the Galicians and Asturians. The Celts who settled in England also used their horses to improve many of the British pony breeds. They soon established trading routes between northern Iberia and England or Ireland.

At this time, there is no evidence linking any of these breeds to the modern Andalusian or Lusitano, but breed purity and registries are relatively modern. In earlier times, there may well have been some crosses between these two types of horses. Sylvia Loch is an internationally known authority on Spanish horses. She believes such crosses may explain why the dished face of the Garrano occasionally appears in the southern breeds.

The Spanish Andalusian, the Portuguese Lusitano, and Sorraia

The other type of horse shown in the cave paintings originally lived in the fertile valleys of the Tagus River in Portugal and the Guadalquivir River in Spain. Until recent times, the Spanish Andalusian and the Portuguese Lusitano were the same breed of horse. From these southern centers, this type spread throughout Iberia. It probably began with the Sorraia or a similar type of wild horse, but soon became the Iberian Andalusian. Modern DNA analysis has shown the Iberian Andalusian is closely related to the Barbs of North Africa. Some experts believe the equine species initially migrated to Africa from Iberia while others believe the migration went from Africa to Iberia. They agree horses have often been moved back and forth between these two geographic areas. What has been ignored ignore is the actual date when the land bridge permanently disappeared.

Five million years ago, the Mediterranean Sea did not exist. Instead a deep valley linked the two continents and a barrier held out the Atlantic Ocean. The existence of this bridge is one of the reasons why there are so many similarities between the plants and animals found in southern Spain and North Africa. Most experts agree horses crossed back and forth over this barrier or bridge; but when it existed, the true horse (Equus Caballus) had not yet evolved. After it eroded or broke, water flooded into the deep valley. With water this deep, glacier shrinking was not enough to ever bring the bridge back.

After this bridge disappeared, equine migrations between Iberia and North Africa had to wait until horses had been domesticated and could be shipped back and forth by humans. The Straits of Gibraltar are not shallow, but they are less than nine miles wide. Horses could swim across them, but there is no record showing humans driving them through the water.

The Sorraia has recently been recognized as one of the ancient Iberian breeds. In medieval times, it was called a zebro in Portugal and a Marismeno in Spain. In the 20th century, a few were discovered in wild herds and some dedicated horsemen set out to restore this primitive breed. They hypothesized it could well have been one of the prehistoric ancestors of the Andalusian, the Lusitano, and possibly the Barb. Although the tarpan is now extinct, other experts believe it is the remote ancestor of the Iberian horse. Attempts have been made to recreate it by breeding back from modern horses. The Sorraia and the Tarpan share the same primitive colors and have other characteristics in common.

Modern DNA analysis has established the Sorraia carries a unique set of maternal genes. No similarities were found between them and the Spanish Andalusian, but in modern times, the Spanish have introduced both Arabs and Throughbreds into their bloodlines. The

Portuguese have stayed much closer to the classic type of Iberian horse and the Lusitano does share one of its mare lines with the Sorraia. Author Arsenio Raposo Cordeiro describes some Sorraias who still work as cow horses in Fontalva, but they were not included in this DNA research. Whether or not the Sorraia was the prehistoric ancestor of the Iberian horse, the cave paintings show animals with similar characteristics.

Shown below are the heads of a Sorraia stallion, a Lusitano stallion, and a Lusitano mare. Iberian breeds typically have an olive shaped eye and a straight or convex profile.

Domestication and Specialized Breeding

Considerable controversy exists over when humans domesticated the Iberian horse. A cave painting dated 5,000 BC shows humans leading horses. Most experts agree domestication occurred between 4000 and 6000 BC, but others argue that it occurred much earlier. To support their theory, they describe the large quantity of halberds and lances with counterweights found in prehistoric sites. These weapons are normally used by mounted cavalry. So far, no evidence has been found to indicate any use of chariots in Iberia.

In Iberia, horses of the southern type have traditionally been used for hunting, herding cattle, and war. All of these tasks require a handy horse who can easily be collected. Selective breeding for horses with these abilities may have begun as soon as they were domesticated. By 2000 BC, what evolved is a horse who is naturally balanced and readily works off his hindquarters. According to Author Sylvia Loch, by then they had the characteristics listed below.

a) Head – slightly convex or straight profile, olive shaped eyes, and relatively long ears.
b) Neck – powerful, set deep at the base with natural arch. Heavy forelock and mane.
c) Withers – Relatively high.
d) Body – short coupled with wide powerful loins. Rib cage is deep and inclined to be flat. Back appears rounded. Sloping croup with low set, heavy tail.
e) Hind legs – positioned well under the body to produce excellent hock action and forward impulsion.
f) Gaits - powerful, lively, and springy with rounded action.
g) Hooves - small, round, and high.
h) Constitution - strong, hardy, and does well on modest feeding.
i) Temperament - courageous, level headed, anxious to please, easy to train, and gentle.

Most of these characteristic are shown in the three photographs below and on the next page. A Lusitano stallion is shown below. On the next page is another Lusitano stallion and a Lusitano filly. Lusitanos are used as examples because the Portuguese did not introduce either Arab or Thoroughbred blood into their modern horses, as did the Spanish.

According to Author Juan Llmas, the canon bones of all Iberian horses should be rounded in front. This rule applies to all four legs. Under their forelocks, some Spanish Andalusians have a small, round hole in their skull where once a horn could have grown. The first Andalusian I saw had this characteristic. Some like to believe this feature suggests there might have been unicorns somewhere in their ancestry.

After 2000 BC, the Phoenicians and later the Carthaginians settled in southern Spain. They soon began crossing their Oriental horses with the native stock to develop what became known as Andalusians. What they brought with them to Spain could not have been the Arabian because this breed did not yet exist. As late as classical times, the Arabs rode camels.

The Oriental horses they used came to ancient Persia from Turkemenia. When they reached Mesopotamia, the Assyrians further developed this ancient breed before Phoenician traders introduced it all along the African coast. Oriental blood gave the Iberian horses more refinement and size, but did not change their basic conformation. The common people mostly continued to use the hardy, inexpensive native stock while the Iberian Andalusians became the mounts of choice for the nobility.

Summary:

For thousands of years two different types of horses have coexisted in Iberia. The northern breeds are the Garrano, Galician, and Asturian. They are related to the British pony breeds and have had little impact on the southern breeds. These breeds are the Spanish Andalusian, Portuguese Lusitano, and Sorraia. Some experts believe the Sorraia was the ancient ancestor of the Andalusian, Lusitano, and Barb. Others give this honor to the tarpan.

In Iberia, horses were domesticated as soon as 6,000 BC and used for hunting, herding cattle, and war. What evolved was a naturally balanced horse who readily works off his hindquarters. Well before the birth of Christ, the nobility used Oriental blood to give some of the native horses more size and refinement. At that time, the Spanish Andalusian and the Portuguese Lusitano were still the same horse.

Myths:

The true origin and much of the history of the Iberian Andalusian has been obscured by the mists of time. From time to time, experts have developed different theories about the history of the Iberian horse, but when verifiable facts contradict such a theory, it becomes a myth. Two such myths have been identified in this chapter.

Myth One:

115

Most experts still believe the genetic relationship between the Iberian Andalusian and the North African Barb was created when wild horses crossed the land bridge between North Africa and Spain, but true horses had not yet evolved when this bridge was permanently destroyed.

Myth Two:

Many believe the good qualities of the Iberian horse came from the Arabian. Some Oriental blood was used to create the Iberian Andalusian, but it came from the Turkmenian horse, not from the Arabian. As late as classical times, the Arabs only rode camels.

Acknowledgements:

Photographs 1-3, 6, and 10 are courtesy of Wikipedia. Permission to use photographs 4-5 was given to me by Galicenos of Suwannee Horse Ranch near Live Oak, Florida.

Iberian Horses
Chapter 11: Historic Legacy

The Spanish Andalusian and the Portuguese Lusitano shared the same origins and prehistoric history. Unlike the Arab and the Thoroughbred, they were bred to work off their hindquarters. When they went to war or faced the ferocious Iberian cattle, this ability served them well. Instead of racing across the relatively flat deserts of Arabia or the green turf of England, they had to travel over uneven ground on the mountains, hills, and plains of Iberia. The Iberian cavalry amazed the known world with their ability to travel over rough ground and climb or descend mountainous slopes.

Classical Outflow

By classical times, all the lands around the Mediterranean Seas had heard of the quality of Iberian cavalry. They used the ginete style of riding with a bent knee. Despite their excellent riding and weapons skills, their success depended on their fast, agile, highly trained horses. Author Sylvia Loch suggests they may have already begun using stirrups made out of simple loops of rope.

Mercenaries from Iberia helped Sparta defeat Athens and the Carthaginians defeat Rome. One of their techniques was to gallop towards their foe, execute a quick stop, throw their javelins, then spin their horses around and take off before their opponents had time to react. To achieve the required quickness and speed, the horse had to work off his hindquarters. The harmony between these men and their horses impressed many and some believe the legend of the centaur was created to describe them.

When the Romans adopted Iberian tactics and weapons, they had to learn to wear light armor, ride ginete style, and grip with their knees. They set up stud farms are over Iberia and used Iberian horses to improve their cavalry stock. They did bring a few Camargue horses to Iberia who may have been bred to Iberian horses. Their remount stations sent horses throughout their empire where Iberian horses may have been used to improve the local breeds.

The Conquest of Iberia - Barbs and Andalusians

DNA research has established the Barb and the Iberian Andalusian are closely related, but there is considerable controversy over when and where this relationship began. Many experts have assumed the genetic relationship between these two breeds was first created when wild horses crossed the land bridge between North Africa and Andalusia, but this bridge was destroyed before true horses had evolved. This fact proves these two breeds became related much later in time. This relationship could have come from common ancestors or from interbreeding after the Moors invaded Iberia. Both of these breeds may have been affected by the early importation of Oriental horses from Turkmenia.

In 711 AD, Moorish mercenaries came from North Africa to invade the Visigoth states of Iberia. At this time, some still believe the Iberian Andalusian did not exist, but historical evidence has established it had been created by 2,000 BC. One of the invaders, Tarif Ben Tarick, stated the Spanish horses were both bigger and better than their Barbs. To win battles, they had mount their infantry on captured horses.

Some still believe the Moors created the Andalusian when they crossed their Arabs on the cold blooded native horses, but there is no evidence to support theory. For centuries, the Oriental Arab and the African Barb have been misclassified as the same breed, but they have little in common. At the time of the invasion, the Arab breed had just been established and only a few purebreds existed in Arabia. What the Moors brought with them were Barbs. The Norse Dun has often been identified as the native breed, but it never existed in Iberia. The Vikings did settle in France, but only raided into Iberia and North Africa.

During the Moorish occupation, the records show few horses were shipped into Spain, but many were shipped out of Spain. These facts suggest the impact of the Barb on the Andalusian horse has been greatly overstated by most equestrian historians. The Moors did do some crossbreeding, but they used the Andalusians to upgrade their Barbs.

After the Reconquest - Barbs and Andalusians

Although the Iberian Andalusian and the North African Barb do have much in common, they are two different breeds. Francois Gueriniere was a riding master who served Louis IX of France and is thought to be the founder of classical dressage. He knew both breeds well. In 1733, he describes the Iberian Andalusian

"as the best of all horses for the manege [dressage arena], by reason of their agility, strength, and the natural cadence of their gaits; and for processions and parades, due to their proud air, grace, and nobility; and for war on a day of battle because of their courage and obedience."

When he compares them to the Barb, he says

"Barbary horses are cooler in temperament and less graceful of gait; but ...they are well-sinewed, agile, and capable of considerable endurance. They succeed perfectly in the airs above the ground and ... are excellent stallions for the breeding of hunting horses."

In the Ottoman empire, for centuries Arabian horses could not be exported legally, but they could be used to upgrade horses within the Empire. When they eventually reached North Africa, they had some influence on the Barb horse. In Gueriniere's time, the Barbs he knew may have carried some Arabian blood.

The photograph below and the two on the next page are of Barbs. They all have the short back, sloping croup, and low set tail of the true Iberian horse. The one below is of a modern Barb from Morocco.

In the late 1800's, an American cavalry officer traveled from Morocco to Constantinople and wrote a book about what he saw. He took the two photographs, the one below and the one on the next page. The one without a rider appears to be a true Barb. It was taken in Algeria. In the next one, the horse does have a slight dish to his face. It was taken in Tunisia. The closer the author got to Egypt, the more Barbs he found who showed some Arabian characteristics.

Fighting the Moors

For almost eight hundred years, the Spanish and Portuguese fought to drive the Moors out of Iberia. Their long battle begin about four hundred years before knighthood flowered in England, France, and Germany. In these countries, knights in heavy armor learned to ride strong horses in tournaments and into battle. They rode in a style called a la brida with long stirrups and a straight leg. Their style of riding and fighting never reached as far as Iberia.

Bullfighting on horseback or rejoneo began just before the Moors invaded Spain. By this time, stirrups had been discovered and could be used to give the rider better balance, as well as more reach and power. Rejaneo has always been done using the gineta style of riding. It was an excellent training exercise to prepare men and horses for battle. It honed the fighting skills of men, but also encouraged them to breed faster, handier, and braver horses. These fights were an indirect factor, but a major one in the improvement of the Iberian Andalusian.

The Moors on their swift, streamlined horses were not easy to defeat. To win against them in the hot Iberian climate, warriors had to use a minimum of armor, lighter weapons, and ride gineta style. Since the Moors came in 711 AD, the Iberian warriors probably used Roman armor. The Iberian horses were just as agile as the Barbs, but more powerful. The photo below shows a statue of El Cid on Babieca.

A few Barb stallions might have been bred to Iberian mares to give their offspring more speed and endurance. Although knights in heavy armor stopped the Moors from invading France, they probably could not have driven the Moors out of Iberia. Andalusians may not have been as fast as Thoroughbreds or Arabs over shorter distances, but they have won many endurance races.

Riding a la brida with a straight leg, as the English, French, and German knights did, did not come to Iberia until after the Moors had been driven out. It was briefly used in the practice of the new art of high school dressage, but Iberian horsemen eventually went back to riding only in gineta style.

Reconquest and Outflow

By 1492, the Moors had been driven out of Iberia and the Iberian Andalusian became available for export. They went to the New World and founded many breeds there, as well as to European countries where they became the foundation stock for breeds, such as the Lipizzaner. For several centuries, Iberian Andalusians were in great demand at every court in Europe. They excelled at the new art of dressage where their ability to collect served them well. The two photos on the next page first show a modern Lusitano, then a modern Lipizzaner.

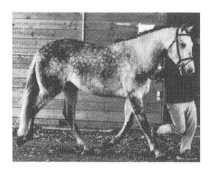

The unique features of the Iberian horses have made them difficult to classify. When the Europeans finally developed three categories to describe all breeds of horses, the Iberian horses fit into none of them. These categories are hot bloods, cold bloods, and warm bloods. Only Arabs and Thoroughbreds are hot bloods. The Iberian horse existed long before either one of these breeds was created by humans. They are level headed horses who can control their hidden fire (brio condido). Cold blooded horses have never existed in Iberia because they use oxen or mules for heavy work. Iberian horses are only allowed to pull carriages. One author suggests some of the pony breeds may belong to cold blood classification, but the Iberian pony breeds derive from the Garrano who lived in prehistoric times. If the Iberian horses are not either hot or cold bloods, then they cannot be classified as warm bloods who mix hot and cold blood.

They are unique and need a special classification of their own.

In the centuries after the Reconquest, some changes did affect the Iberian horses. When the king of Spain stopped bull fighting on horseback (rejaneo), breeders began breeding a new type of Andalusian, one with a longer back and higher stepping gait. Rejaneo continued in Portugal, but gradually became more moderate and less dangerous. Breeders there kept right on producing the compact classical Iberian horse. Late in the nineteenth century, rejaneo came back to Spain and to get more speed, they breed Arabs and Thoroughbreds to their horses. These crosses could legitimately be called warm bloods.

Summary:

By classical times, the excellence of the Iberian cavalry and horses had been well established. They used the gineta style of riding with a bent knee. The Romans turned Iberia into a breeding farm and spread the Iberian horse throughout their empire. When the Moors invaded Iberia in 711 AD, they brought a few Barbs with them, but made extensive use of the native Andalusians. In the long fight to expel the Moors, the sport of bullfighting on horseback or rejonero was used as a training exercise for both men and horses. After the Reconquest, Iberian horses spread to the New World and other European countries where they founded many new breeds. The classic Iberian horse is relatively unique. He is not a hot blood, cold blood, or warm blood.

Myths:

The true origin and much of the history of the Iberian Andalusian has been obscured by the mists of time. From time to time, experts have developed different theories about the history of the Iberian horse, but when verifiable facts contradict such a theory, it becomes a myth.

Myth One:

Many believe the Moors brought the gineta style of riding with them to Spain, but the Iberians used this style long before the invasion and have always used it for bull fighting on horseback (rejaneo).

Myth Two:

Many believe the Moors brought Arabs into Spain and used them to create the Iberian Andalusian; but at the time of the invasion, the Arabian breed had just been established. When it did reach North Africa, it was used to improve the Barb, but not the Iberian Andalusian.

Myth Three:

Many believe the Iberian warriors fought in heavy armor and on heavy horses, but the knightly style of riding never reached Iberia. Their warriors rode gineta style and used smaller, handier horses. Because they rode gineta style, some call their horses jennets or ginetes.

Myth Four:

Many still believe the Iberian breeds are warm bloods. They predate the development of the breeds classified by Europeans as hot bloods or cold bloods. Nonexistent breeds could not be crossed to create warm bloods.

Acknowledgements:

Photographs 4 and 6: Courtesy of Wikipedia.

Iberian Horses
Chapter 12: The Long Journey Home

The Journey

When the Spanish came to the New World, the only domestic animals they found here were dogs and llamas. They had to bring horses, cattle, sheep, goats, and pigs first to the Caribbean Islands and from there to the Americas. To the Conquistadors, warhorses were the most critical items. For the settlers, all of these species were essential. Where ever they found suitable land, they set up cattle ranches and used horses to herd, round up, brand, and kill their cattle.

On his second voyage in 1493, Christopher Columbus brought horses for the first time to the New World. Shipment after shipment followed. These animals were not always of the highest quality and only the toughest could survive the long and arduous voyage. As the crow flies, Iberia and the Caribbean were over four thousand miles apart.

In the days of sailing ships, voyages between the Old and New Worlds were only feasible because of the trade winds. To reach the New World, Spanish galleons first had to sail south to Madeira or the Canary Islands. After picking up fresh food and water, they could sail west by catching the easterlies. To return to the Old World, they had to sail north to pick up the westerlies. There are romantic stories about survivors from shipwrecks reaching the eastern coast, but they are myths. The Spanish had no reason to return horses to Spain, ships wrecked on the northeastern route would not have had horses with them.

In the sixteenth century, voyages from Spain to the Caribbean could take two to three months and the loss of animals often exceeded fifty percent. Horses were shipped two different ways, both of which prevented them from moving. In the hold, they were locked into stalls and on deck, they were hobbled and tied. The horses on deck could be swept overboard in a storm. The drawing below shows a horse in a sling who has been locked in a shipping stall.

The Spanish galleons were square rigged ships who sailed best with the wind. When the winds were favorable, they could make up to eight knots or about nine miles per hour. If they got too close to the Equator, they could be caught in a calm and forced to throw animals overboard to conserve water. On his first voyage, Columbus took five weeks to travel from the Canary Islands to San Salvador in the Bahamas. A Spanish galleon is shown below.

The Spanish records generally showed how many stallions and mares were shipped, but not what breed or type they were. They probably included Andalusians, Sorraias, Garranos, Asturians, Galicians, and other ponies. For centuries, the Spanish had used pack ponies on the southern slopes of the Pyrenees Mountains. Some believe a few Pottok or Basque ponies were included in shipments to the New World. Pintos are common in this breed.

Since there are almost no historic records of what mixtures of types actually reached which locations, we can only guess at what their foundation stock may have been by examining the breeds that emerged there. For example, some experts believe South America received more Sorraias than did North America.

The Islands

The four largest islands in the Caribbean are Cuba, Hispaniola (Santo Domingo), Jamaica, and Puerto Rico. In 1493, Columbus brought both horses and cattle to Hispaniola. Horses were soon shipped to other islands. They reached Jamaica and Puerto Rico in 1509, as well as Cuba in 1511. These islands soon became home to hundreds of horses, many of whom worked on the ranches. The map below shows Spanish territories as of 1513.

From the Islands, horses were soon shipped to both continents and the isthmus between them. Horses reached Panama in 1512, Mexico in 1519, and Columbia in 1524. Although more horses kept coming from Spain, the conquistadors preferred the native horses who had been born in the New World and had already begun adapting to their new environment. The horses Cortez and Desoto brought to the mainland came from Cuba. When Pizarro set out to conquer the Incas in 1832, his horses came from Jamaica, Panama, and Mexico.

By 1520, the horse population had expanded so fast the emperor forbad sending anymore horses to the New World. After that date, any exports required special permission and extensive paperwork. Special horses were sometimes sent to upgrade the quality of the horses in the New World. By 1550, outstanding horse breeders were found in Santo Domingo, Jamaica, Mexico, and Nicaragua. The horses they produced went both north and south and are still being used throughout Latin America.

Timeline

1493   Columbus brings first horses to Santo Domingo
1509   First horses arrive in Jamaica and Puerto Rico
1511   First horses arrive in Cuba
1512   First horses arrive in Panama
1519   Cortez lands in Mexico with horses from Cuba
1520   Emperor stops automatic shipments of horses to the New World
1532   Pizarro sets out with horses from Jamaica, Panama, and Mexico

Breeding in the New World

Multiple factors influenced the types, breeds, and qualities of the early Iberian horses in the Americas. Four have already been discussed and are listed below.

129

1) What types of horses were shipped here from Iberia.
2) What horses survived the brutal voyage.
3) What types of horses were shipped to which Islands in the Caribbean.
4) What types of horses reached the mainland.

Two additional factors are environmental adaptation and selective breeding. In the New World, breeders had to work with whatever horses survived and thrived in their location. They had to breed for type to recreate all of the desirable qualities of the various Spanish breeds. These breeds did not include Arabs. Today there are Spanish Arabs, but they did not exist during the time of the Conquistadors. For centuries, the Ottoman empire forbade the export of any purebred Arabs.

Many erroneously believe the North African Barb was one of the Spanish breeds shipped to the New World. The Andalusians do carry some Barb blood in their heritage, but the breeders could not have imported any for their breeding programs. When the Moors were driven out of Spain, they left no Barbs behind them. The Ottoman Empire had strict laws controlling the export of any of their horses. The Spanish also enforced strict laws on what could be imported into their Empire. For centuries after the Reconquest, corsairs from the Barbary States of North Africa plagued the western Mediterranean and controlled access to their coasts. In the nineteenth century, the United States fought two wars with them.

Breeding for type began early. Horses were bred for war, games, herding cattle, endurance, parades, and ambling gaits. On the Islands, the emerging breeds fell into three general categories. Warhorses, criollos, and pasos. The conquistadors wanted good warhorses, but they were not always available. Andalusians had been bred for war and games, but few had been included in the first shipments to reach the New World. The criollos herded cattle and had great endurance. Criollo simply means native or born in America. The pasos had ambling gaits, made delightful riding horses in rough country, and looked well in parades.

In South America, the extensive importation of non-European breeds did not begin until after they had thrown of Spanish rule early in the nineteenth century. Evaluating what had evolved in Latin America prior to this time can give us some clues as to what equine breeds reached where in the New World.

The First Horses

In 1519, Cortez arrived in Mexico with seventeen horses. They were described from memory by one of the Conquistadors as shown below.

Capt. Cortez had a dark chestnut stallion who died when we reached San Juan Ulua.

Pedro de Alvarado and Hernando Lopez de Avila had a very good bright bay mare, who turned out excellent both for tilting and for racing. When we arrived in New Spain [Mexico] Pedro de Alvarado took his share either by purchase or by force.

Alonzo Hernandez Puertocarreo, a grey mare. She was fast, and Cortes bought her for him for a gold shoulder knot.

Juan Velasquez de Leon, another grey mare, and she was very strong. We called her "La Rabona" [bob-tailed].

Christoval de Olid had a dark brown horse that was very satisfactory.

Francisco de Morla, a dark bay horse which was very fast and well reined.

Francisco de Montego and Alonzo de Avila, a dark chestnut horse; he was no good for war.

Juan de Escalante, a light bay horse with three white stockings. He was not very good.

Diego de Ordas, a grey mare. She was barren and a pacer, but not very fast.

Gonzalez Dominguez, an excellent horseman, had a dark brown horse, very good and very fast.

Pedro Gonzalez de Trujillo had a good bay horse, a beautiful color, and he galloped well.

Moron, a settler of Bayamo, had a pinto with white forefeet and he was well reined.

Baena, from Trinidad, had a dark roan horse with white patches, but he proved worthless.

Lares, a fine horseman, had a good horse, bay in color, but rather light; he was an excellent galloper.

Ortiz the musician and Bartolome Garcia, who had gold mines, had black horse called "El Arriero" [Drover] and he was one of the best horses that we took aboard the fleet.

Juan Sedeno, from the Havana, a brown mare, and this mare had a foal on board ship. This Juan Sedeno was the richest soldier in the fleet, for he had a ship, a mare, a negro, and much cassava bread and bacon.

These seventeen horses were the first ones to return to North America. They are mixed in both type and quality as were all the horses imported to the Islands by the Spanish.

Conclusion:

When horses returned to the New World, they first had to survive a long and arduous voyage. Even when the Spanish galleons caught the trade winds, the trip could still last for two to three months. Over half of the horses died on the journey. The small tough pony breeds and the Sorraias probably had a better chance of surviving than did the bigger, finer Andalusians.

The Spanish kept no records to tell us what breeds of horses they actually shipped or which ones reached which islands in the Caribbean. They probably send Sorraias,

Garranos, Asturians, Galicians, and a few Andalusians. From the Islands, they spread throughout North and South America. After their arrival at their final location, environmental adaptation and selective breeding affected the way they developed.

By 1520, the King forbad the shipment of horses to the New World. After that date, horses could still be shipped, but special permission and reams of paperwork were needed. Wealthy landowners and breeders did import Andalusians to upgrade the creole or native breeds.

Myths:

The true origin and much of the history of the Iberian Andalusian has been obscured by the mists of time. From time to time, experts have developed different theories, but when verifiable facts contradict such a theory, it becomes a myth.

Myth One:

Some believe the romantic stories about horses surviving shipwrecks and reaching the shore of North Americas, but the galleons were sailing back to Spain and would have no reason to take horses with them.

Myth Two:

The Iberian Andalusians and the North Africa Barbs are related, but this relationship may well have been created before the Reconquest in 1492. In my opinion, the export laws of the Ottoman Empire, the import laws of the Spanish Empire, and the activity of the Barbary corsairs would have prevented the export of any Barbs from Spain to the New World.

Acknowledgements:

Spanish Horsemen and Horses in the New World

Map by Santus, courtesy of Wikipedia.

2nd illustration, courtesy of Wikipedia.

Iberian Horses
Chapter 13: The Criollos (Creoles)

Where ever the Spanish had established cattle ranches, criollo horses were used to handle the herds on the open ranges. Like creole, criollo simply means native or born in America. When applied to horses, it is a generic term like warmblood. In South America, cowboys are not called vaqueros and their name varies with the location. For example, in Argentine they are called gauchos.

The foundation stock for the criollo breeds was probably Sorraias with the addition of a few Andalusians. The ranch owners and managers preferred to ride the better examples of this breed. Today criollos are recognized in the modern countries of Argentina, Brazil, Chili, Columbia, Peru, and Venezuela. In the other countries of Latin America, criollos may still work cattle where ever there are ranches who need them.

Before the South American Revolutions, the Spanish colonies were divided into four viceroyalties - New Granada, Peru, Chili, and Rio de la Plata. New Granada included the modern countries of Panama, Columbia, Ecuador, and Venezuela. Rio de la Plata included the modern countries of Argentina, Bolivia, Paraguay, and Uruguay. The map on the next page shows them in the eighteenth century. Next to Venezuela, is the Dutch colony of Guyana and the French colony of Suriname. The large blank area is what became Portuguese governed Brazil.

In Latin America, criollos can be found where ever there are cattle to work. They share the basic Iberian characteristics listed below. As compared to Andalusians, some criollos do have shorter heads. This feature may have come from one of the pony breeds or from Barb genes carried by Andalusians.

1) Head with straight or convex profile.

2) Thick, abundant forelock, mane, and tail.

3) Neck muscular and often has rounded crest.

4) Strong, slopping shoulders.

5) Short back with well sprung ribs and wide, powerful loin.

6) Well muscled hindquarters with sloping croup and low set tail.

7) Strong legs with good bones and well developed joints.

8) Hard feet with thick walls.

9) Healthy, disease resistant, and known for great endurance.

10) Height varies with location. Average 13 to 15 hands.

A common criollo shows the characteristics described above in the photo below.

Depending on the location, environmental adaptation and selective breeding have created some minor variations in their appearance. Criollos have had to adapt to life in the Andes mountains, the pampas (prairies), and the savannahs of the northwestern coast.

Criollos - Peru

When Pizarro set out to conquer the Incas, he brought some good horses with him and used them to terrorize the Indians. After the Inca empire had been destroyed, the wealthier colonists, who came directly from Spain, brought many fine Andalusians with them. Peru soon became a center for distributing horses throughout South America.

The Peruvian criollo is a special breed which has adapted to life at high altitudes with minimal feed. This breed has two distinctive types. The common one is the Andean (Andino or Morochuco). Their average height is from 12 to 13.2 hands. The are used as pack ponies and riding horses. Their habitat is at an altitude of over nine thousand feet. As a result, they have developed a extra lung capacity and dense coats. They are expected to carry over two hundred pounds as they climb steep hills at altitudes up to sixteen thousand feet.

Unlike the Andeans, the Chumbivilcas are small riding horses, who live only in Cuzeno and Apurimas. Their average height is 14.1 hands. They are more developed than the Andian and are used by army because of their strength, agility, and adaptation to high altitudes. Both the Andeans and the Chumbivilcas are paso gaited, but they do not have the status of the showy Peruvian Paso.

Criollos - Chile

In 1541, conquistador Don Pedro de Valdivia brought the first horses to Chile and more horses soon followed. Most of them came from the province of Charcas in Peru, but fine stallions were gathered from many locations. Colonists soon established ranches in the fertile valleys and began breeding horses. Their horses were never allowed to run free and did not have to adapt to tropical climates, poor feed, or high altitudes. From the beginning, breeders placed great emphasis on the quality of the horses their programs produced. By 1610, they had earned a reputation for breeding the best horses in South America.

The Chilean criollo is known as the corralero. It was initially bred for stock work and sprint racing, but found an excellent market in the military. Due to Chile's remote location, there were no early imports of European breeds. It was a closed breed type and formal registration began as early as 1893. In modern times, it found a new role in rodeo competitions. The photograph below shows a huaso (gaucho) on his corralero, standing in a wheat field.

The photos below and on the next page show three Chilean criollos owned by Antilco, Pucon, Chile. The third horse is a mare. This farm offers horseback riding adventures in the mountains of southern Chile.

A genetically unique breed lives on the island of Chilote off the shore of southern Chile. They are the only confirmed pure descendants of the horses brought to America by the Conquistadors. No other breeds have ever been imported to the island.

These small horses show some Spanish characteristics. At twelve hands, they are pony sized, but act more like horses. Their size could represent environmental adaptation, but also could have come from the import of the Iberian pony breeds. They are ridden, carry packs, and pull carts. A Chilote pony carrying double is shown below.

The Pampas

The pampas of South America are grasslands like our prairies. Both provide ideal conditions for equine survival. When Spanish horses reached our prairies, the feral population expanded by leaps and bounds. The same phenomena occurred on the pampas. The true pampas cover 300,000 square miles and include northeastern Argentina, all of Uruguay, and the northeastern corner of Brazil. This term has also been used to describe the grasslands of Patagonia and Paraguay, as well as the savannahs of Venezuela.

Criollos - Argentina

Buenos Aires sits in an optimal area for colonization. The central pampas contain some of the best farm land in the world. It is fertile and well watered by the Rio de la Plata and its tributaries. In 1535, Don Pedro Mendoza founded a colony there. He brought with him a shipload of purebred Iberian horses from Cadiz, Spain. In 1541, hostile Indians forced the Spanish to abandon their colony. Before leaving, they turned seven mares and two stallions loose on the pampas.

Buenos Aires was resettled in 1580 by pioneers from Peru. They came down out of the Andes, through the deserts, and across the arid areas in western Argentina. They estimated 12,000 feral horses had survived on the central pampas. In addition to horses from the failed colony, their ancestors probably included strays or escapees from Peru and Chili. Since the settlers came from Peru, Lima was their only legitimate port. Smuggling began early and only stopped when the viceroyalty of Rio de la Plata was created in 1776.

Patagonia lies south of the true pampas and is a semi-arid grassland. As settlements expanded and the feral herds grew in number, they had to move south. Adaption to that environment created a tough horse who could survive extreme cold and heat, scanty water, and live on dry grasses. These horses were the foundation stock for the criollo breed. A photograph of a gaucho riding a criollo is shown below.

In North America, feral horses are called mustangs. In South America, they are baguales. During the six years of the first Buenos Aires colony, the local Indians quickly learned how to handle and ride horses. After the Spanish left, they caught and tamed baguales to ride and use as pack animals. When the Spanish returned, the gauchos had to imitate them. The first criollos were wild horses they caught, tamed, and trained. The photo below is of a herd of criollos in Patagonia.

As compared to the criollos in other areas, the ones in Argentina were thickset and stocky. Some believe their ancestry may have included some Garrano ponies. Like ponies, they live longer than most horses do. Others suggest their build reflects a reversion to original species of the wild horses from Eurasia. There is some evidence to support this theory. The original baguales were reddish brown or bay, as were the first true horses.

As this breed evolved, dun and grulla coloring became common and popular with the gauchos. They believed this coloring went with exceptionally tough horses with great endurance. Horses with these colors may have a stripe down their back, one across their shoulders, and stripes on their legs. This coloring points to a strong Sorraia heritage, as does the smaller size of the earlier criollos.

Criollos have fantastic endurance. Gauchos felt a horse who could not consistently travel sixty miles a day and go two days without food or water was useless. There are many authenticated stories describing the fantastic endurance of these horses. Some examples are given below.

1) In 1810, Major Corvalan rode the same horse from Buenos Aires to a town situated at the foot of the Andes. They covered 665 miles in five days, averaging 133 miles per day.

2) From 1925 to 1928, Aime Tschiffely rode two criollos, Mancha and Gato, from Buenos Aires to New York. They both lived until they were 40 years old.

3) In 1993, Vladimir Fissenko and the criollo, Sufridor, traveled from Tierra del Fuego to Deadhorse, Alaska. They spent five and one-half years on the journey.

In the nineteenth century, many European horses were imported and crossed on the native breeds. In 1918, the breeders in Argentina decided to create a criollo registry, but a major conflict broke out over the definition of a true criollo. By 1934, Dr. Emile Solanet had gained control. He used the Chilean criollo as his standard and introduced rigorous endurance tests to select acceptable horses for breeding.

Criollos - Other

As the pampas stretch north from the central area, they become increasingly dry. They include both Uruguay and the northeastern corner of Brazil. The criollos from Uruguay are thought to be similar to the ones from Argentina. Their registry began in 1929 and in 1941, breeders formed a society to protect the purity of their breed.

In Brazil, the criollo is known as the Northeastern (Nordestino), Crioulo Brasileiro, Curraieiro, or Sertanejo. This breed is small, averaging 13 to 13.2 hands, and may be descended from the Garrano pony and the Sorraia. It has adapted well to a harsh environment and developed an immunity to ticks. Where most horses will starve, it will survive by eating harmful weeds, cogon grass, and bitter grasses. In recent years, it has been neglected and decimated. An association is working on maintaining and improving it.

For almost all Latin American countries, the extensive importation of European breeds did not begin until after they had thrown off Spanish rule early in the nineteenth century. Brazil is the exception. The Dutch colony of New Holland controlled much of the Brazilian coast from 1581 to 1654 and they imported many horses from the Low Countries and southwestern Germany. The Friesland horse could be the one who introduced paint coloration into Brazil.

Venezuela lies on the northern coast of South America. The Llanero plains are mostly treeless savannas covered with swamp grasses and sedges. The Llaneros are also known as the Venezuelan Criollo or Prairie Horse. Their average height is 14 hands. They live in a hotter climate than do the Argentina criollos and have adjusted by becoming both smaller and less stocky. They are also paso gaited.

Conclusion

The main ancestors of the criollos were probably the Andalusians and Sorraias, but they also share some of their characteristics with the pony breeds. Although the Sorraias were smaller, both breeds had the classic Iberian conformation. The Andalusians were medium sized, compact, agile, handy, and built for collection, carrying men in armor, and surviving on minimal feed. The nobles used them mainly for war and fighting savage bulls. What the Iberian vaqueros used for herding cattle was mostly Sorraias. This cross produced excellent cow ponies with great endurance. What the pony breeds may given some of the criollos was a smaller size, a longer life, more muscling, and paso gaits.

Acknowledgements:

Antilco, Pucan, Chile has given me permission to use the three photos of their Chilean Criollos.

Map of South American by Jluis, courtesy of Wikipedia.

Photos 1-2, 7 courtesy of Wikipedia.

Iberian Horses
Chapter 14: The Paso Gaited Horses

Paso simply means step. Paso horses do not trot because they are born with a natural four beat gait. Their special gaits are smooth and easy for the rider to sit. Some criollos have these gaits and may be more closely related to the pasos than are the criollos who do not have them.

The Asturian is the ancestor of all the easy gaited horses in Iberia and the New World. They were well known in classical times and called Asturcones. When they were exported in medieval times, they were called haubvini in France, palfreys in England, and hobbies in Ireland. In medieval times, jennet or ginete was initially used to describe any Spanish riding horse, some of whom were gaited. This term derived the gineta style of riding. In the time of the Conquistadors, Andalusian stallions were bred to the small gaited mares to produce what they called jennets. Today that term has come to mean only horses with easy gaits.

Unlike the criollos, the pasos do not exist in all of Latin America. Breeding for their special gaits began early in the Islands. Pasos soon spread to the northeastern coast, and followed Pizarro to Peru, but they never moved south into countries like Chili, Argentina, or Uruguay. Pasos can be divided into three general types. The first one has showy gaits and has less endurance. The second ones are ordinary riding horses with easy gaits and more endurance. The third one combines easy gaits with working cattle.

Paso Finos

Asturians probably came with some of the first shipments to the Caribbean. When they were bred to Andalusians, the result was a Paso Fino. Paso fino means fine step. Different lines developed in Santo Domingo, Cuba, Puerto Rico, and Columbia, but all lines of Pasos exhibit the same type of lateral gait. Environmental adaptation and specialized breeding explain why the lines diverged at various locations.

In Puerto Rico, breeders wanted a showy horse with a great deal of style. Their gait can be executed in thee speeds, the paso fino, paso corto, and paso largo. The paso fino is a showy gait. In the paso corto, the horse moves at the same speed, but it is more relaxed and used as a trail gait. The paso largo is the extended form of the paso fine and is very fast. There are ranches in Puerto Rico, but their paso finos are not normally used for cattle work. The two photographs below show a Paso Fino moving under saddle and naturally.

In Columbia, breeders wanted an easy gaited horse who could be used to work cattle. The Colombian criollo is also known as the Colombian Paso Fino or the Colombian Walking Horse. The Colombia patriots naturally believe their horse is the best, the purest, and the most unique of the Paso breeds. They have an elegant and noble appearance and show great brio in their way of going. A horse with brio shows vigor, spontaneous spirit, and fire. He is also easy to control and exceptionally responsive to his rider. The photograph below is of a Columbian Paso Fino.

Pasos from all locations and lines have been imported to the United States and Europe. In an attempt to improve quality, breeders have crossed them. Some attempts are now being made to maintain or restore the bloodlines of each individual line.

Peruvian Pasos

Unlike other Latin American countries, Peru did not develop a livestock-based economy. In the north, overseers of the vast sugar or cotton plantations had to go long distances. In the deserts of the south, only sturdy horses could survive long trips through it. Both types needed good endurance, but not the speed or agility required for working cattle.

The Conquistadors probably bought with them some horses who had already been bred for gait. When more Andalusians were imported directly from Spain to Peru, they were bred to them. The result was horses who did a paso llano or the sobreandando. Of the two, the paso llano is the slower gait and the one generally used for riding cross country.

When the Viceroyalty of Peru was established in 1542, the demand for showy horses increased. More imports created a handsome horse who was both taller and heavier than the Paso Finos. The Peruvian Pasos were bred for brio and an additional feature in their gait. They had to show termino, an outward swinging action of the forelegs.

The two photographs below show a Peruvian Paso in traditional equipment and in motion.

Brazilian Pasos

In 1581, the Dutch began settling along the coast of Brazil and importing horses from northern Europe. When formally ceded their land to Portugal in 1661, the Portuguese settlers had to import Spanish horses from neighboring colonies. In 1740, the Lusitano stallion, Sublime, arrived from Portugal. When bred to gaited mares, he founded a new breed, the Mangalarga Marchador.

These handsome horses combine docility and endurance with two easy gaits, the marcha batida and the marcha picada. They are both lateral and diagonal gaits. The difference between them is defined by the moment when they have three feet on the ground. Their fast, smooth gaits make them good horses for riding long distances and they also excel at working cattle. Two of them are shown below.

End Note: Iberian Breeds Today

The evaluation of the Iberian breeds in South America has established their ancestors were probably Andalusians, Sorraias, Garranos, Asturians, and Galicians. The mixture of types appears to have varied considerably with the location of the native breeds. It was also affected by whether they were criollos, pasos, or shared the heritage of both types.

Comparisons between modern Iberian breeds has one basic limitation. Over five hundred years has passed since horses arrived back in the New World. Beginning towards the end of the nineteenth century, the bloodlines of various European horses was introduced into the Spanish breeds in Spain and South America. One example of what happened is in the history of the Peruvian Paso. To improve termino, they bred Hackneys, Thoroughbreds, and other breeds to their horses.

DNA research has been done on some of the criollo and paso breeds. They belong to the general Spanish group, but have stronger genetic relationships with each other. This finding may have been partially caused by the inclusion of the pony breeds in what was shipped to the New World. The analysis of South American breeds also shows a high level of diversity. There could be more than one reason for this diversity. It could reflect the crossing with various European bloodlines, but also the ancient origin of some of the horses brought to the New World.

Conclusion

The pasos first emerged on the Islands where Andalusian stallions were bred to mares who had inherited their easy gaits from Asturians. This cross spread throughout the Islands and the northern coast as far south as Peru, but never reached as far as Chili or Argentina. The small size of breeds like the gaited Chilote pony and the Brazilian Nordestino suggests there were one or more of the pony breeds in their ancestry.

Acknowledgements:

Photos 1, 3-5 courtesy of Wikipedia.

Spanish Horses
Chapter 15: From Louisiana to Virginia

When the Spanish discovered the New World, they found no horses here. They first shipped horses to the Caribbean Islands and from there they went west to Mexico and north to the Gulf coast and Florida.

Whenever the Spanish expanded their holdings, typically the explorers came first, then the missions, and finally the ranches. The friars always brought animals with them and trained the local Indians in animal husbandry and agriculture. They followed this pattern to establish themselves in Mexico and what would become our southeastern states. Where ever the Spanish explorers, friars, or colonists went, they took horses with them, most of whom came from one or more of Caribbean Islands.

In the early fifteen hundreds, the Spanish began exploring and settling in the southeast. By 1565, they had established their first permanent settlement in St. Augustine, Florida. The horses in this area arrived in more than one way.

Arrival and Development

1) From the Southwest?

Some believe the southeastern Indian tribes got their horses from the southwestern tribes, but the Spanish horses did not reach that area until well after they had already been established in the southeast. Since the Indians only had canoes, they probably had no effective way to get horses across the Mississippi River. By the mid eighteen century, the English colonists had begun importing mustangs with a Spanish heritage from the southwest.

2) Expeditions (Strays?)

Regardless of where the Spanish expeditions went, they rarely left any strays behind them. Horses were valuable and closely watched. The expeditionary records showed which ones were killed in battle, eaten, or brought back by the expedition. Since Spanish gentlemen did prefer to ride stallions, they took few mares on their expeditions. There were few strays and they would probably have been killed and eaten by Indians or predators, such as wolves.

3) Failed colonies (Marsh Tackies)

Failed colonies may have eaten their horses, taken them back with them to one of the Islands, or left some stock behind them. Colonists always wanted to expand their herds and flocks as soon as possible so their foundation stock included many females and few males. In 1521, when Juan Ponce de Leon made an abortive attempt to establish a colony in Florida, he brought fifty horses with him. After his colony failed, the surviving horses may have been returned to Cuba or left behind.

In 1526, Lucas Vazquez de Ayllon made another attempt to establish a colony near the Santee River in South Carolina. He also brought stock with him, including eighty-nine horses. After fever had killed most of the colonists, the survivors fled, but left their animals behind. These horses are thought to be the ancestors of the Marsh Tackies.

This breed of tough, small, gaited horses has adapted well to the hot, wet low country of eastern South Carolina. During our Revolution, they were used by Francis Marion, the Swamp Fox. They still excel as mounts for swampland hunters. This breed survived well into the twentieth century and a registry for them was established in 2007. A photograph of a modern Carolina Marsh tacky is shown on the next page.

4) Shipwrecks (Banker ponies)

Various romantic legends claim horses escaped from shipwrecked Spanish galleons and reached shore. Many galleons did founder along our southeastern coast, but there is no evidence that any of these home bound treasure ships carried horses. While the Spanish shipped many horses to the Caribbean, they would have had no reason to send any of them back to Spain.

However, there was one real case of shipwreck survivors. In 1585, Sir Richard Grenville picked up stock, including horses in Cuba. When his five ships ran aground on Wococon (present day Oracoke Island), the horses may have been the first to swim to shore. In a letter to Sir Francis Walsingham, Grenville suggested that some of the livestock survived on this island. These horses are thought to be the ancestors of the wild horses who still live on the offshore islands of North Carolina's outer banks. Today there are ponies on Shackleford, Corolla, Ocracoke, Core, Hatteras, and Cedar Islands. Two photographs of modern banker ponies are shown below and on the next page.

5) Spanish Missions (Florida Crackers)

Today most historians believe most of the southeastern horses came from the Spanish missions. Florida did not become American territory until 1822. Before that time, it included a narrow strip of land that spread west along the coast to the borders of French Louisiana. The Spanish started missions all along this coastal strip and both the Choctaw and Creek Indians got horses from them.

Spanish missions eventually spread as far north as Charleston. One was established in Virginia, but didn't last long. Northern Florida and southern Georgia were called the Spanish Guale. By 1650, it contained seventy-nine missions, eight large towns, and two royal ranches. Strays from their horse herds probably mingled with the Marsh Tackies and banker ponies.

Beginning in 1565, the Spanish settled most heavily in Central Florida where they established ranches for Spanish cattle and horses. To do their job, cow ponies have to have cow sense, agility, early speed, and endurance. For centuries, the Spanish horses had been bred for these qualities. They gave them to the modern breed, the Florida Cracker Horse. Like the Marsh Tackies, they are gaited. In 1895, Frederick Remington drew a picture of a Cracker cowboy on his horse. It is shown on the next page and followed by a photograph of a modern Florida Cracker.

When the last remnant of the coastal missions retreated back to St. Augustine in 1706, they left behind tribes, such as the Cherokees and Chickasaws, with many fine horses. Strays from mission or Indian herds are thought to be the source of the feral herds that plagued the English colonists in Virginia and the Carolinas. They began complaining in 1670.

A Lost Breed: The Chickasaw Horse

The English colonists didn't know the local horses were not native, but descended from the horses brought by the Conquistadors. They believed they were Indian ponies and called them, Chickasaws, despite the fact the five civilized tribes all had horses. These tribes were the

Cherokees, Chickasaws, Choctaws, Creeks, and Seminoles. They had their own herds, but they also caught and tamed many feral horses for sale to the back country traders. Whether the traders bought or stole them, they used Indian ponies to bring their peltry to market before they sold them to the colonists.

In his early history of South Carolina, Dr. David Ramsay commented that the Indian ponies were handsome, active, hardy, but small; seldom exceeding thirteen and one half hands. The mares in particular, when crossed with English blooded horses produced colts of great beauty, strength and swiftness. James Adair, a South Carolina trader, commented the Cherokees had a prodigious number of excellent horses and were skillful jockeys.

Chickasaw horses were short and chunky, closely coupled, quick to action, but not distance runners. In the early days, the colonists ran their horses in match races for a quarter of a mile. The Chickasaws did well in these races and are thought to be part of the foundation stock for the modern Quarter horse. Chickasaws were probably bred to Hobbies from Ireland or Galloways from Scotland to create the first quarter horses.

Later in the eighteenth century, the addition of Thoroughbred blood turned these sprinters into the colonial quarter race horse. When Thoroughbred racing started in the colonies, quarter racing did not die; it just moved away from the coast and continued on the frontiers.

Chickasaws were extremely popular in South Carolina. When settlers began moving into Tennessee, they came closer to the Chickasaw homeland and continued to value, use, and breed Chickasaws. They also took them with them when they settled in Texas.

When the southeastern tribes were forced to go to Oklahoma, they did bring their horses with them. The Chickasaws lost many horses to American and Indian thieves. Except for the Choctaws, the tribes did not keep records or try to maintain any unique strains in their herds.

In the United States today, there are still breeders who have horses who are descended from the original Spanish stock. They are known Colonial Spanish Horses. Their general characteristics are the same as for the Latin American criollos. DNA analysis has confirmed the Marsh Tackies, the banker ponies, and the Florida crackers all belong to this horse group. The original Chickasaws certainly would have been part of it, but their identity was lost when they were crossed with too many other breeds.

Conclusion:

From the Caribbean Islands, the Spanish spread to what would become our southeastern states. They established missions on a strip of land along the Gulf Coast, in Florida, and up the eastern coast as far north as Virginia. They brought horses with them and taught farming and ranching to the Creek, Choctaw, Seminole, Cherokee, and Chickasaw tribes. The Marsh Tackies, the banker ponies, and the Florida Crackers have been recognized as Spanish Colonial horses. The English colonists called the horses they found here Chickasaws. This breed has lost their identity because they crossed so well with horses imported from England.

Acknowledgements:

Photographs 1-2, 4-5, courtesy of Wikipedia.

Spanish Horses
Chapter 16: From Vera Cruz to the Rio Grande

In 1519, Hernan Cortez brought horse from Cuba to Mexico. As the Conquest continued, more horses arrived from Santo Domingo and Cuba. Once the Aztecs had been defeated, the Spanish took over their land and used much of it for ranching. New Spain eventually came to include south Texas, Arizona, New Mexico, and California.

New shipments of horses from the Caribbean to Mexico included some Andalusian warhorses and many Sorraias. By 1550, breeding farms in Chiapas and Nueva Valladolid were known for the quality of the horses they produced. The finer the horses, the more highly they could be trained for the upper classes and the military.

The Mexican Criollo and Azteca

The Spanish in Mexico used the open range style of ranching. To handle the wild and ferocious Spanish cattle, they need excellent cow ponies. Horses were also raised on the open ranges and some turned feral. Once feral herds were established, more horses were lost to them. The word, mustang, derives from the Spanish term, mesteno. It means a wild horse or cow. The hacendados soon began crossing Andalusians, Sorraias, and mestenos to create the Native Mexican Horse. In this context, native means criollo or born in the Americas.

Like all the criollo breeds of South America, the Mexican criollos have an excellent shoulder, short back, strong loins and hindquarters, good legs with plenty of bone, and hard feet. They are also agile, athletic, courageous, and have great stamina.

During the Mexican Revolution, thousands of horses died in battle, but some criollos survived so their breed did not completely die out. In 2004, photographer Bill Wittliff produced a book of photographs showing criollos

160

working on an old fashioned Mexican ranch. Unfortunately, these hard working horses never had an official breed registry.

By 1972, the charros had created a new breed, the Azteca. By breeding back, they believed they could re-create the original horses bred by the early hacendados from the horses bought by the Conquistadors. They also wanted to preserve the qualities of the criollo, but in a bigger, more attractive horse. To achieve their goal, they crossed imported Andalusians on criollo and quarter horse mares. The Quarter Horse they choose to use probably carried little Thoroughbred blood. By this time, the Andalusians had long since split into two types. What they probably used was old type stallions who had been bred for performance. The Azteca is now the national horse of Mexico and rigorous inspection standards are used to maintain the breed standards in Mexico. Below are photographs of two Mexican Aztecas.

The Azteca horse has become popular in the United States. The American registry does not allow criollo bloodlines, but will accept paints. Unlike Mexico, they do not have inspection standards. The two photographs on below show two Aztecas from this registry.

The Mexican Galiceno

Along with many Sorraias and some Andalusians, a few Garranos, Asturians, and Galicians also reached Mexico. The Galiceno pony lives in a remote costal area of Mexico and DNA research has shown their closest relatives are the Garrano ponies. Since they are gaited and the Garrano is not, they are probably also descended from the Asturian. Their name suggests they are also related to the Galician. Both the Asturian and the Galician are thought to be descended from the Garrano.

Beginning in 1958, Galicenos have been imported into the United States and they qualify as one of the Colonial Spanish Horse breeds. The Suwannee Horse Ranch in Florida has given me permission to use the photographs their Galicenos below and on the next page.

The picture above was taken at Mission San Luis in Tallahassee, Florida. The riders are wearing what soldiers wore there in 1703.

Galicinos are either solid colors or roans. Pinto or appaloosa color patterns are not acceptable. They do produce duns with primitive markings, such as the one

163

shown below. This mare has the back stripe and the shoulder markings, but no stripes on her legs above her black stockings. This coloring, along with their Spanish characteristics, does suggest Galicinos may also have some Sorraias in their ancestry.

Conclusion:

As the Spanish settled in the southeast, they were also advancing through Mexico to what would become our southwestern states. Breeders in Mexico created the perfect cowpony in the native (criollo) Mexican horse. In the twentieth century, the charros imported Andalusians and crossed them with both mustangs and the remnants of the criollo. The result was a new breed, the Azteca. The Galiceno pony had long lived in a remote costal region of

Mexico and was gaited. In recent years, some have been imported to the United States and recognized as Spanish Colonial horses.

Acknowledgements:

Photographs 1-2, courtesy of Wikipedia
Permission to use photographs 5-8 was given to me by Galicenos of Suwannee Horse Ranch near Live Oak, Florida.

Spanish Horses:
Chapter 17: West of the Mississippi

Spanish missions and settlements in Mexico gradually moved north towards the Rio Grande River. By 1598, Spanish settlements had reached the borders of New Mexico; but settlement in Texas did not begin until 1690. When the Spanish fled from Santa Fe after the Pueblo revolt in 1680, they left behind hundreds of horses. When historians found none of the Plains tribes had horses until well after this date, they decided these horses were the most probable source of the herds of feral and Indian horses who roamed our western plains in the eighteenth and nineteenth centuries.

The Mustangs

As compared to the Argentine pampas, our prairies were a more ideal environment for horses. In both locations, the feral population mushroomed rapidly and early travelers reported the same problems with the hordes of friendly, curious feral horses. They had to somehow get past the feral herds while keeping their tame horses from escaping to join them.

Like the Argentine criollos, the mustangs became well known for their exceptional endurance. Author Colonel Richard Irving Dodge once tried to buy a good looking pony for $40, but his price was $600. His owner was an express rider who carried mail between Chihuahua and El Paso. Traveling at night to avoid the Apaches, every week he and his pony took three days to cover the three hundred miles between the two cities. After six months of this work, his pony was still sound and in good condition.

As compared to the first horsemen, the southern Plains Indians had several advantages. The Spanish taught them how to ride and care for horses and they stole broke mounts from them. This process was repeated as northern tribes without horses learned and stole from the ones who already had them.

The Indians gradually adapted Spanish techniques and equipment to their needs. They used their best horses as war ponies or buffalo runners while the others moved their belongings by travois or packhorses. According to author John C. Ewers, each Indian family needed a minimum of twenty horses and some had more. The drawing below shows an Indian hunter on his pony spearing a buffalo.

By the time the expanding United States had reached the prairies, Indian warriors become superior horsemen who spent most of their days on horseback and rode ponies who had adapted well to this harsh environment. Military men described them as the finest light cavalry in the world.

How the West Was Won

On the eastern coast, colonists soon began to import various breeds or types of horses from England or Europe. These bigger horses did well in the fertile lands east of the Mississippi River, but did not function well on the prairies. They needed grain to stay in good condition and travel any distance. The US cavalry choose to use bigger horses because each cavalrymen had one horse who had to carry him and a considerable amount of equipment. To keep these horses in good condition, they had to ship large quantities of grain, often for long distances. Even with grain fed horses, the cavalry normally traveled only twenty miles per day.

Unlike the cavalry, the early American explorers, trappers, and cowboys had to ride the tough little Spanish ponies. The explorers and trappers purchased most of their horses from one or more of the Indian tribes. At times, they may also have been forced to catch and break feral horses. The cowboys also had to ride grass fed horses, but they each had more than one horse to ride. Whenever a horse grew thin and tired, he was simply turned back out on the range for a rest.

When American began arriving in Texas, they had to bring horses with them, purchase them from the Spanish hacendados, or catch mustangs. The Chickasaw horses from the Carolinas generally made good cow ponies, but other eastern breeds usually lacked both agility and cow sense. When American ranchers needed horses, they purchased them from the Spanish hacendados. Both the Chickasaw and Mexican horses descended from breeds who had been used to work the ferocious Spanish cattle for hundreds of years in Spain. In Mexico, the hacendados had bred for horses who excelled at handling cattle of the open ranges of northern Mexico. They were tough, agile, smart, and brave. These qualities served them as well in what became Texas.

There are two drawings on the next page by Jo Mora. The first one shows an early American vaquero on a Spanish pony. The second one shows a cow crowd in the years 1867-1880 when most cowboys still rode Spanish ponies. The horses in this drawing were taller, probably because they had received better nutrition in their early years.

Early Texan
Cowman on his little
Spanish paint pony.

1867-1880 Southwest Texas. A cow crowd - brush poppers of the Brasada

Mustangs Versus Ranchers

As long as their stock has plenty of grass and water, ranchers may choose ignore the feral herds, but whenever they need more range for their stock, their solution has always been to catch and sell or kill wild horses. As the American ranches expanded, the wild horses had to go.

Historically many various abusive methods have been used to catch wild horses. When a draught hit California, the hacendados sent their vaqueros out to kill

169

mustangs by driving them into the ocean or off cliffs. They also trapped them into corrals and ordered them to be killed or simply allowed to die of thirst. The drawing below by Jo Mora shows the results of one of the killing drives.

At times of severe drought, hundreds of roving mesteños, unbranded and unknown, were destroyed to conserve pasture

In the open range style of ranching, horses could all too easily turn feral and join the wild herds. Wild stallions also increased their harems by stealing domestic mares. In the early days in Texas, the mustangs mostly carried Spanish bloodlines. As other breeds reached the prairies, some escaped and joined the wild herds.

170

Before the Americans drove the Mexican ranchers out of Texas, they rarely tried to catch mustangs. Afterwards, they could no longer easily buy Spanish ponies so they had to rely on trapping mustangs. The male horses were gelded, broke to ride, and used as cowponies. When the railroads reached far enough, they were also sold to the eastern markets. The mares were bred to stallions with European bloodlines to get bigger horses or to donkey jacks to get mules.

At the beginning of the nineteenth century, an estimated one to two million mustangs lived on the prairies. By the end of the century, this situation had changed. The Indian herds had been decimated as the tribes were forced onto reservations. Like the buffalo, the mustangs had to be killed off to open up the ranges for settlement. During the Boer War of 1899-1902, the British bought and shipped thousands of mustangs to Africa.

When horse meat could be sold to the canning industry, catching mustangs became a profitable business. Remnants of the wild herds were pushed into more and more inhospitable country. In the 1950's, a public campaign began to save what was left of the wild herds. In 1971, a new law put the federal Bureau of Land Management in charge of the few thousand remaining mustangs. When horses are acquired through their adoption program have been tamed and trained, they have usually turned out to be fine mounts for their owners.

Remnants of the Spanish Horses:

At the beginning of the nineteenth century, the horses in the west generally descended from Spanish stock. They were usually described as Indian ponies or American mustangs. In the twentieth century, men who had used and admired these tough little horses began a long and successful campaign to find and preserve the remnants of the Spanish horses. They derived from the five breeds who had been brought here by the Conquistadors. Some of these horses had Asturian ancestry and are gaited. Multiple registries have emerged; and in their search for the pure Spanish horse, each one has set up different registry requirements. When they are grouped together, they are known as Colonial Spanish Horses. The photographs below show three common types of Colonial Spanish horses. They illustrate how the multiple breeds who came with the Conquistadors had adapted to new environments.

The first one is the southern or Sorraia type. Horses who live in hot climates are typically smaller and more refined than the ones who must survive our northern winters. This filly is owned by Marye Ann Thompson from Apache Trail Ranch in Arizona.

The second one is an example of the huskier northern type. He is owned Wes Thompson of Zen Cowboys in Minnesota. This handsome horse was born outside on the coldest day ever recorded in Minnesota.

The third photograph is of the classic Iberian type. I purchased him from Kim Kingsley of Horse Head Ranch in North Dakota and found photographs of Lusitanos and Andalusians who look very much like him.

Conclusion:

When the Spanish fled from Santa Fe after the Pueblo revolt in 1680, they left many horses behind. Currently historians agree these horses were the original source of both the feral herds and the Indian ponies who inhabited on our prairies. Before the Americans reached the West, the Indians had become superb horsemen. They sold or gave their tough ponies to the early explorers and trappers. The Texas cowboys first acquired them from the

173

Spanish hacendados and later from the wild herds. In the twentieth century, men who knew and valued the Spanish horses, hunted for the few survivors of this breed, gathered them together, and started various breed registries for the Spanish Colonial horse. Remnants of the wild herds now contain few examples of the old Spanish bloodlines are currently managed by the Federal Bureau of Land Management.

Myths:

The true origin and much of the history of the Iberian Andalusian has been obscured by the mists of time. From time to time, experts have developed different theories about the history of the Iberian horse, but when verifiable facts contradict such a theory, it becomes a myth.

Myth One:

Many still believe only one pure Spanish breed came to the New World, but the Conquistadors brought multiple breeds or types of horses with them. The Spanish Colonial Horse includes many different genetic mixtures who may come from anyone or more of these breeds. The only "pure" Spanish horses today are the ones living on Chilote Island.

Acknowledgements:
The drawing of the Indian killing buffalo is used with the permission of Candace Liddy.
The three drawings (17-19) by Jo Mora are used with the permission of the jomoratrust.com.
Permission to use the photograph of a southern type was given to me by Marye Ann Thompson of Apache Trail Ranch.

Supplemental Material

Myths

The true origin and much of the history of the Iberian Andalusian has been obscured by the mists of time. From time to time, experts have developed different theories about the history of the Iberian horse, but when verifiable facts contradict such a theory, it becomes a myth.

Myth One:

Most experts still believe the genetic relationship between the Iberian Andalusian and the North African Barb was created when wild horses crossed the land bridge between North Africa and Spain, but true horses had not yet evolved when this bridge was permanently destroyed.

Myth Two:

Many believe the good qualities of the Iberian horse came from the Arabian. Some Oriental blood was used to create the Iberian Andalusian, but it came from the Turkmenian horse, not from the Arabian. As late as classical times, the Arabs only rode camels.

Myth Three:

Many believe the Moors brought the gineta style of riding with them to Spain, but the Iberians used this style long before the invasion and have always used it for bull fighting on horseback (rejaneo).

Myth Four:

Many believe the Moors brought Arabs into Spain and used them to create the Iberian Andalusian; but at the time of the invasion, the Arabian breed had just been established. When it did reach North Africa, it was used to improve the Barb, but not the Iberian Andalusian.

Myth Five:

Many believe the Iberian warriors fought in heavy armor and on heavy horses, but the knightly style of riding never reached Iberia. Their warriors rode gineta style and used smaller, handier horses. Because they rode gineta style, some call their horses jennets or ginetes.

Myth Six:

Many still believe the Iberian breeds are warm bloods. They predate the development of the breeds classified by Europeans as hot bloods or cold bloods. Nonexistent breeds could not be crossed to create warm bloods.

Myth Seven:

Some believe the romantic stories about horses surviving shipwrecks and reaching the shore of North Americas, but the galleons were sailing back to Spain and would have no reason to take horses with them.

Myth Eight:

The Iberian Andalusians and the North Africa Barbs are related, but this relationship may well have been created before the Reconquest in 1492. In my opinion, the export laws of the Ottoman Empire, the import laws of the Spanish Empire, and the activity of the Barbary corsairs would have prevented the export of any Barbs from Spain to the New World.

Myth Nine:

Many still believe only one pure Spanish breed came to the New World, but the Conquistadors brought multiple breeds or types of horses with them. The Spanish Colonial Horse includes many different genetic mixtures who may come from anyone or more of these breeds. The only "pure" Spanish horses today are the ones living on Chilote Island.

Information Sources:

Chapter Nine:

Anthony, David W. "The Origins of horseback riding", Antiquity 65, 1991, pp. 22-38.

Baumann, Deb. "Are Wild Horses Really Wild?" Equestrian News, June 2006.

Dawal Cai. "Ancient DNA provides new insights into the origin of the Chinese domestic horse", Journal of Archaeological Science, volume 36, issue 3, March 2009, pp. 835-842.

Dodge, Theodore A. "Riders of Syria", New Monthly Magazine, Oct. 1993, pp. 771-8.

Edwards, Elwyn Hartley. The New Encyclopedia of the Horse. London, Dorling Kindersley, 2000.

Harrigan, Peter. "Discovery at A-Mager", Aramco World, May/June 2012.

Hayes, Capt. M. Horace. Points of the Horse, 7th edition. NY, Arco Publishing Co., 1969. Pp. 300-309.

Hendricks, Bonnie. International Encyclopedia of Horse Breeds. Norman, OK, University of Oklahoma, 1995.

Jansen, Thomas. "Mitochandrial DNA and the origins of the domestic horse", Proceedings of the National Academy of Scientists, v. 99, no. 116, Aug. 6, 2002, pp. 10905-10910,

Kirkpatrick, Jay. F. Into the Wind: Wild Horses of North America. North Word Press, Minocqua, Wisconsin, 1994.

Ladendorf, Janice. "Equine Evolution", Valley Equestrian News, August, 2015, pp. 8, 10, 12.

Levine, Marsha A. "Domestication, Breed Diversification and Early History of the Horse", McDonald Institute for Archaeological Research, Cambridge, UK. Presented a Workshop on Horse Behavior and Welfare, June 2002.

MacLean, Mac. "Local tarpan [Hengart Stroebel] herd relocate to southeast Oregon", Bend Bulletin, Oct. 6, 2013.

Orlando, Ludovic. "Recalibrating Equus evolution using the genome sequence of an early Middle Pleistocene Horse", Nature 499, July 4, 2012, pp. 74-8.

Pynn, Larry, "Genetic study of Chilcotin's wild horses finds surprising links to Siberia", Vancouver Sun, Jan. 7, 2015.

Raff, Lynn. "Spirit Horse: Equus Przewalski: Ancient Ghost of the Steppes". Art Horse Magazine, Winter 2010, issue 10, pp. 4-11.

Vila, Carles. "Widespread origins of domestic horse lineages", Science, Jan. 19, 2001, pp. 474-7

Warmuth, Vera M. "Reconstructing the origin and spread of horse domestication in Eurasian steppes", Proc. of the National Academy of Scientists, v. 109, issue 21, May 22, 2012, pp. 8202-8206.

Warmuth, Vera M. "Ancient trade routes shaped the genetic structure of horses in eastern Eurasia", Molecular Biology, v. 22, issue 21, Nov. 2012, pp. 5340-5351.

Chapter Ten:

Bastos-Silveria, Luis C. "A lost Sorraia maternal lineage found in the Lusitano horse breed", Journal of Animal Breeding and Genetics, v. 123, #6, Dec. 2006, pp. 399-404.
Cordeiro, Arsenio Raposo. Lusitano Horse: The Son of the Wind, Lisbon, 1991.
D'Andrade, Fernando. A Short History of the Spanish Horse and of the Iberian "Gineta" Horsemanship for Which this Horse is Adapted. Lisbon, 1973.
Hayes, Capt. M. Horace. Points of the Horse, 7th edition. NY, Arco Publishing Co., 1969, pp. 300-309.
Hendricks, Bonnie. International Encyclopedia of Horse Breeds, University of Oklahoma, 1995.
Interagro Lusitanos, "The Origins and Evolution of the Lusitano", www.lusitano-interagro.com.
Ladendorf, Janice. "The Lusitano Horse, pt. 1, May 2015, pp. 8-10.
Llamas, Juan. This is the Spanish Horse. J. A. Allen, 1997.
Loch, Sylvia. The Royal Horse of Europe. J. A. Allen, 1986.
Royo, L. J. "The Origins of Iberian Horses Assessed via Mitochondrial DNA", Journal of Heredity, Nov.-Dec. 2005, pp. 663-669.

Chapter Eleven:

Cordeiro, Arsenio Raposo. Lusitano Horse: The Son of the Wind, Lisbon, 1991.
D'Andrade, Fernando. A Short History of the Spanish Horse and of the Iberian "Gineta" Horsemanship for Which this Horse is Adapted. Lisbon, 1973.
Denhardt, Robert M. The Horse of the Americas. University of Oklahoma Press, 1949.
Dodge, T. A. Riders of Many Lands. NY, Harcourt, 1894.
Ferguson, Robert. "When Allah Met Odin", pp. 246-262, The Vikings, Penguin, 2009.
Gueriniere, Francois. Ecole de Cavalerie, 1733, p. 39.
Hyland, Ann. Equus: The Horse in the Roman World. Yale University Press, 1990.
Ladendorf, Janice. "The Lusitano Horse, pt. 2", Valley Equestrian News, June, 2015. pp. 12-13.
Llamas, Juan. This is the Spanish Horse. J. A. Allen, 1997.
Loch, Sylvia. The Royal Horse of Europe. J. A. Allen, 1986.

Chapter Twelve:

Denhardt, Robert M. The Horse of the Americas. University of Oklahoma Press, 1949.
Hendricks, Bonnie. International Encyclopedia of Horse Breeds, University of Oklahoma, 1995.
Loch, Sylvia. The Royal Horse of Europe. J. A. Allen, 1986.

Chapter Thirteen:

Cunninghame, Graham R. B. The Horses of the Conquest. University of Oklahoma, 1949.
Denhardt, Robert M. The Horse of the Americas. University of Oklahoma Press, 1949.
Hendricks, Bonnie. International Encyclopedia of Horse Breeds, University of Oklahoma, 1995.
Loch, Sylvia. The Royal Horse of Europe. J. A. Allen, 1986.

Chapter Fourteen:

Cothran, E. G., "Genetic analysis of the Venezuelan criollo horse", Genetics and Molecular Research vol. 10, no. 4, 2011, pp. 2394-2403.
Denhardt, Robert M. The Horse of the Americas. University of Oklahoma Press, 1949.
Dent, Anthony and Machin-Goodall, Dalphene. The Foals of Epona, 1st edition, Galley Press, 1962.
Hendricks, Bonnie. International Encyclopedia of Horse Breeds, University of Oklahoma, 1995.
Kelly, L. "Genetic characterization o the Uruguayan Creole horse and analysis of relationships among horse breeds.", Research in Veterinary Science, vol. 72, Feb. 2002, pp. 69-73.
Loch, Sylvia. The Royal Horse of Europe. J. A. Allen, 1986.
Luis, C. "Iberian origins of New World horse breeds", Journal of Heredity, March-April, 2006, pp. 107-13.
Mirot, P. M., "Phylogenetic relationships of Argentinean Creole horses and other South American and Spanish breeds inferred from mitochondrial DNA sequences", Animal Genetics, vo. 33, Oct. 2002, pp. 356-53.
Cunninghame, Graham R. B. The Horses of the Conquest. University of Oklahoma, 1949.
Denhardt, Robert M. The Horse of the Americas. University of Oklahoma Press, 1949.
Hendricks, Bonnie. International Encyclopedia of Horse Breeds, University of Oklahoma, 1995.
Loch, Sylvia. The Royal Horse of Europe. J. A. Allen, 1986.

Chapter Fifteen:

Adair, James. History of the American Indians. London, 1775, pp. 230-32.
Chard, Thornton. "Did the first Spanish horses landed in Florida and Carolina Leave Progeny?" American Anthropologist v. 42, Jan-March 1940, pp. 90-106.
Denhardt, Robert M. Quarter Horses: A Story of Two Centuries. University of Oklahoma, 1967, pp. 18-81.
Dunham, Wally. "The Chickasaw Horse", Western Horseman, Oct. 1963, pp. 26, 97.
Haines, Francis. Horses in America. Ty Crowell Co., 1971.
Howard, Robert West. The Horse in America. Follett Pub., 1965.
Ladendorf, Janice. "A Lost Breed: The Chickasaw Horse", Valley Equestrian News, July 2014, pp. 8-9.
Ramsay, Dr. David. History of South Carolina, 1809, p. 403.
Roe, Frank Gilbert. "The 'Stray' Legend", The Indian and the Horse. University of Oklahoma, 1974, pp. 33-55.
Smith, Alexander Mackay. The Colonial Quarter Race Horse, 1983.

Chapter Sixteen:

Denhardt, Robert M. The Horse of the Americas. University of Oklahoma, 1947.
Hendricks, Bonnie. International Encyclopedia of Horse Breeds, University of Oklahoma, 1995.

Chapter Seventeen:

Denhardt, Robert M. The Horse of the Americas. University of Oklahoma, 1947.
Dobie, J. Frank. The Mustangs. University of Texas, 1984.
Dodge, Col. Richard Irving. Our Wild Indians: Thirty-Three Years of Personal Experience Among the Red Men of the Great West, 1st published in 1884. NY, Archer House, 1959, p. 587.
Ewers, John C. The Horse in the Blackfoot Indian Culture. Smithsonian Institution Press, 1955.
Hendricks, Bonnie. International Encyclopedia of Horse Breeds, University of Oklahoma, 1995.
Loch, Sylvia. The Royal Horse of Europe. J. A. Allen, 1986.
Lowe, Percival G. Five Years a Dragoon (1849-54) and Other Adventures on the Great Plains, University of Oklahoma, 1965.
Ryden, Hope. America's Last Wild Horses, Lyons & Burford, 1990.
Wittliff, Bill. Vaqueros: Genesis of the Texas Cowboy. University of Texas, 2004.

Book 3: Historic Fiction

Morzillo
The Horse Who Became A God

Cuba, 1519

Men brought my ancestors across the ocean from Spain to the New World. As a colt, I had heard many tales of their sufferings and about all the horses who died on the journey. I shuddered every time I thought of a horse being thrown overboard to the sharks waiting below.

I had been born on an island our masters called Cuba and expected to stay there. Every stallion wants his own harem of mares. I worked hard for my owners, but dreamed about someday becoming a ranch stallion like my sire.

One day, my worst nightmare came true. My two owners brought me to a wharf and asked me to stand in a row of strange horses. While I drew their scents into my nostrils, one of my masters ran a sling underneath my body. I reared and tried to twist away from it, but both men swung on my lead rope and brought me back down to the ground.

Other men hooked ropes to the sling before they hauled me up into the air and down into the hold of a ship. My trip through the air left me too shaken to resist any further. Men left the sling around me and hung it from the deck above me. They encircled my body with poles and hobbled my right front foot to a ring bolted to the deck.

Men soon lowered other stallions into the hold to share my captivity. We asked each other where the ship was going, but none of us knew the answer. We heard men cheering on shore, thumps on the deck above us, and soon afterwards the ship began moving. As it surged through the water, I swung back and forth in my sling and felt it rubbing against the hair on my belly.

182

My sensitive ears soon heard gusts of wind and rain hitting the deck above me. I had lived through many storms, but always with solid ground underneath me. As the motion of the ship grew rougher, I panicked. If it went down, I knew it would take me with it. If I could break out of my cell, then I might be able to swim to shore. I thrashed around, but couldn't get myself loose.

Every time my rump or chest slammed into one of the poles, it hurt me more. We horses sometimes kick each other, but not over and over. Every slam gave me new bruises or deepened old ones.

To keep my balance, I tucked my hindquarters underneath me and kept shifting three of my feet around. All my attempts to move or free my right front foot failed and I soon had a bloody welt above my fetlock joint.

During the storm, men climbed down into the hold and staggered across the deck to bring us food and water. Soon after the storm, the ship stopped moving. We horses could smell land, but men did not release us. None of us horses understood why they wanted to keep us in the hold of this ship.

After a few days, it began crashing through the waves again. To stay healthy, we horses know we have to keep moving. How long did men plan to hold me immobile in this cell? How long could I stay healthy? How long could I bear it? I had tried to free myself, but still could not take even one step forward or back.

I'm a proud and powerful black stallion. I should be leading pack trains to and from the gold mines, not stuck in this hole. Like all stallions, I dreamed about having my own herd of mares and foals to guard, but there were no mares with us in the hold of this ship.

I had two masters, Garcia and Ortiz, and they called me, El Arriero or The Muleteer. On every day of our voyage, Garcia brought me food and water, but sometimes they smelled bad. Only thirst forced me to drink scummy water and often I had to pick out the edible hay and maize from all of the rotten or moldy bits. As my flesh melted away, my once gleaming coat grew dull and itchy.

Ortiz spent more time with me. He liked to groom me, pet me, and scratch my itchy spots. When he sang to me, I always enjoyed listening to the song he had made up about me. When he sang other songs, I often closed my eyes and dreamed about being free to round up mares in a Cuban pasture.

Next to me stood a dark chestnut stallion who belonged to our leader, Captain Hernando Cortez. Ortiz often talked to me about his grandiose plans, but all I understood were the words, gold and glory. Humans may search for them, but they mean nothing to us horses.

I wanted to live, not die on this voyage. One day, Ortiz rubbed my neck. "Arriero, don't despair. Our ship is not crossing the ocean. We went west and are following the coast towards a new land called Mexico."

He had always been kind to me, but had betrayed my trust when he helped other men trap me in this cage. Could I believe him? Every time men opened the hatch above us, I could smell land so I decided he had told me true.

After a few weeks, the motion of the ship stopped again. Teams of men came into our hold. They took away my poles, released my right front hoof, hooked ropes to my sling, and swung me up on deck. I felt glad to be of that cell, but wondered what came next.

Ortiz grabbed my halter and held me while Garcia removed my sling. I aimed several kicks at him, but didn't connect. They led me across the deck and helped other men push me off the ship.

Falling through the air terrified me, but I landed in shallow water. It splashed up around me, but I soon found solid ground for my hooves underneath it. As I plunged through the waves and staggered to shore, sea salt burned into the raw sore on my right front leg.

After being held immobile for so many days, all of us horses were weak and stiff. Garcia let me graze and led me around until I felt more like myself. That night I looked forward to lying down to sleep.

He brought me back to the picket line and rubbed my neck. "We've reached Tabasco. Them Mayas welcomed us, but they don't like us. Tomorrow we're gonna show them they can't defy us Spaniards."

The next morning, Ortiz helped him groom, saddle, and bridle me. Neither man smelled happy. Garcia gave Ortiz my reins and stumped off. I looked after him and Ortiz hugged me. "Don't worry, Arriero. He's not mad at you. Our leader ordered him to go with the infantry today. One of his officers, Alonzo de Avila, is going to ride you into battle. He has more experience and armor to wear."

Ortiz led me over to the other horses and held me while de Avila leaped up on me. I gasped as his weight hit my back. I had never before carried a man in armor. I felt his heavy hands on my reins and he hit my sides with his roweled spurs. I obeyed his rough commands and fell into line just behind Captain Cortez.

We followed him for twelve miles, around a swamp and over broken ground. My new rider did a good job of staying with me, but I had a hard time balancing his weight and staying on my feet.

We reached the battle and I saw hordes of Mayas between us and our infantry. The scents of blood and sweating men filled the air. When the Mayan warriors saw us horses, most of them screamed with fear and ran away.

All I wanted to do was flee from the noise and stinks, but my rider used painful jabs from his roweled spurs to make me charge with the other horses. I had to knock down and trample on the Indian warriors. The squishy feel of their bodies under my hooves felt horrible to me.

By the time my rider let me stop, streaks of foam poured off my exhausted body. When Captain Cortez came up to us, my rider laughed. "We knew those Mayas had never seen horses before. We terrified them just as you planned."

The battleground was close to our camp and he let me walk slowly towards it. When we got there, Ortiz took me and cared for me. Five horses had been wounded in the battle and I watched men sear their wounds with fat taken from the body of a dead Indian. It smelled terrible to me.

A brown mare had foaled on the ship. She had been unloaded with the other horses, but left behind when raced off to battle. That night, she came into heat. I bugled to her and fought my picket rope, but couldn't get loose to go to her. Her squeals and my screams of rage kept everybody awake.

In the morning, her colt wandered off, she started calling for him, and men brought him back to her. Captain Cortez walked up to her, slapped his knees, and laughed. "I have an idea. Bring her over to our meeting place and tie her to the tree behind my chair. Bring Arriero after her."

Garcia untied me, but first ran a chain around my nose and through my mouth. I plunged after the mare, but he didn't let me get close to her until she had been tied to the tree. He let me smell her rump, but refused to let me court her. She kicked out at me, I jumped away, and he dragged me away from her.

When the Indian chiefs or caciques came, I heard a cannon boom and Garcia brought me to their meeting place. The mare was gone, but they tied me to the same tree and her scent still lingered there. I wanted to find her so I bugled and reared.

Captain Cortez grabbed my halter and brought me down to the ground. He laughed. "You are a lusty one."

I saw the caciques trembling with terror. As Garcia dragged me away, I seethed with frustration and anger towards the men who chosen to torment me with a mare in heat.

I did not want to be dumped into the hold of a stinky ship. Instead, I wanted to stay in Tabasco with that mare and her colt, but suspected that our owners would not leave us there. Men did use boats and ropes to drag us horses through the shallow water to it. When I pulled back on my rope, it choked me.

When we got to the ship, I decided to attack the men. One of the sailors leaned over the side of the boat towards me; I sank my teeth into his shoulder, and dragged him into the water. He screamed, but Garcia got him back in the boat. He managed to get the sling around me, but I kicked forward at him and caught him in the belly.

As soon as I felt the deck of our hold underneath my hooves, I reared and lashed out with my front feet, but the men just yanked me back up into the air until they could drop me right down into my cell.

Later, Garcia came to check on me. I laid back my ears and glared at him. He rubbed his belly and laughed. "Arriero, you are a feisty one. I want you to fight Indians, not us Spaniards."

This trip took fewer days. Soon after the ship stopped, teams of men again came into our hold. Impatient for release, I began pawing with my left front hoof. As I landed on the deck, I felt my legs shaking underneath me.

Garcia grabbed my halter and held me while they removed the sling. He led me to the edge of the deck and I saw horses swimming in the deep water. Boats herded them towards shore. That sight didn't scare me because I had swum across many rivers and wanted to reach the land.

This time, nobody had to push me off the ship. I jerked away from Garcia and leaped down into the water. I came back to the surface, swam through the waves, battled through the surf, and reached the sandy shore.

While I shook off the salt water, a servant clipped a lead rope to my halter. He led me to a stream where I had a long drink of clear, clean water. When I lifted my head, I saw him gawking at the men unloading the boats and slack in my lead rope. I leaped into the stream, dropped down, and rolled in the water. It washed the remaining salt out of my coat and soothed my many bruises, cuts, and itches.

The servant yelled at me, dragged me up out of the water, tied me to a picket line, and brought me armloads of fresh cut grass. It smelt sweet and tasted wonderful. I needed lots of good food to regain my health and beauty.

Suddenly, the scent of mares reached my nose. I looked up and saw five of them emerging from the sea. I wanted to run to them, show off, and convince them to admire me. I danced in place and called to them, but they ignored me.

When the Indians came to greet us, they brought many presents with them. They infested our camp and got in the way. Every time they came near one of us horses, I could sense their fear.

These men looked liked the ones who had cared for us horses in Cuba, but those men had never been afraid of us. Since these men acted like the ones in Tabasco, maybe they too had never before seen horses. When men sat on our backs, maybe we looked even stranger to them.

I didn't like this place. We horses had to stand and sweat in the sun. I had trouble breathing the heavy, humid air. Nasty insects tormented both men and horses. When they came at me, I shook my mane, stamped my feet, and swished my tail, but soon itchy bites covered my body.

Several days after our landing, the caciques came to visit us. Garcia hurriedly saddled me and rode me in a demonstration with the other horses in our cavalry troop. As we wheeled and ran together, the bells on our trappings jingled. I had never liked that noise, but had gotten used to hearing it.

When we stopped, I heard a cannon boom while we watched a lovely sorrel mare cavort back and forth on the beach. Her rider shone with pride as he made her race, stop, and spin underneath him. I wanted to run with her, but Garcia used my spade bit to hurt me, hold me, and force me to stand still.

He rubbed my neck and whispered in my ear, "We got them scared good." I didn't like his gloating tone. Every time he flogged one of his Indian workers or servants, I had heard that tone in his voice. My nose told me that the other men had also enjoyed frightening these Indians.

When the show was over, the caciques sent their men off. Soon they returned with maize from their stores and fresh cut grass for us horses. Hungry me had to eat their food, but didn't like the scent of fear that lingered on it.

Captain Cortez gave us horses little time to recover from the voyage. He kept us busy exploring the coastal land and intimidating Indians. From time to time, I felt his greedy eyes looking at me and admiring me. Much to my relief, we soon moved north to a spot with cooler weather and fewer insects.

Before we left the coast, he destroyed our ships. I enjoyed watching them burn because I never wanted to be trapped again in one of those holds.

When everybody was ready to go, he cried, "Onwards to Tenochtitlan," and the men cheered.

Many Indians came with our expedition as guides or servants. They carried heavy loads and waited on our masters. Every time one of us horses whinnied, they hurried to bring us water and food.

As we climbed up from the coastal swamps and jungle, the terrain began to change. All of us enjoyed traveling through the cool pine forests and lush valleys. Many natives lived in those valleys, but small chickens and hairless dogs were the only animals that I saw with them.

We constantly ran into new tribes and tried to impress them, but we could not terrify all of them. The Tlaxcaltecos were the first to attack us with their crude weapons. To defend ourselves and survive, we had to defeat them.

In that battle, I saw a mare get killed when an Indian warrior cut off her head with one stroke and that sight often haunted my dreams. We stallions know that we might have to fight each other to get mares, but none of us understood what benefit humans got from killing each other.

At Zempoala, we fought again. Garcia still had no armor and a spearman got him. When he fell off my back, I stood over him and kept off every warrior that came near us. While I fought on, he bled to death.

After the battle, Ortiz came and led me away. When he had cleaned me up he hugged me and whispered. "Cortes lost his stallion today. He wants to take you and I can't stop him. Unlike me, he can ride you into battle. I wish we had never come to Mexico."

I had heard men call Cortes' stallion vicious, but he told me that he had been taught to be aggressive. Now, I would belong to his owner and wondered how he would treat me.

Cortes gave me a new name, Mi Morzillo or My Black. He was a fine rider, but not a kind man. He used his forceful personality to dominate his soldiers. His horses, he dominated with his skill, a cruel bit, and roweled spurs. Garcia had always made me behave, but Cortes was even stricter with me.

Ortiz had had a loose style of riding that was easy on me and I missed his songs. Even though he no longer rode me, he did visit me often and sometimes I heard him singing around our evening campfires.

As we marched farther into Mexico, we acquired more tribal allies by intimidating or defeating them. Now that our leader rode me, the other horses treated me with more respect, but I continued to dislike the smell of fear that surrounded us and lingered on my food.

When Ortiz stopped coming to see me, I worried about him. I had dreamed that he might someday rescue me from Cortez, but that was before he died from a fever. I missed him and his songs. By then, I knew that Cortez cared only for gold and glory for himself. Often, I dreamed about getting away from him.

Tenochtitlan turned out to be a city built over a lake. The Aztecs welcomed us outside the city. I pranced up to their caciques and felt their admiring eyes on my handsome self.

Cortez dismounted and threw my reins towards my groom. He took them and whispered in my ear, "They think you look like a fabulous black jaguar."

During the ceremony, I used my ears, eyes, and nose to evaluate the behavior of the men. Their scents told me how they felt. Our men reeked of pride and joy while the caciques smelled of fear.

We marched into the city and had to cross the many bridges that spanned the water. The Aztec crowds cheered us, but I could smell their fear and anger. They cried, "Quetzalcoatl." I heard Cortez laugh and laugh. He muttered to himself, "Those stupid savages think I'm one of their gods."

He rode me daily in the city and on a trip back to the coast to pick up more men and horses. When we returned to the city, I saw sullen faces and scented more anger and less fear. Soon the furious Aztecs attacked us and we won some battles, but failed to subdue them.

Where ever we went in the city, a putrid smell soon began to reach my sensitive nose. I had caught the same scent once before. At our gold mine, Garcia had ordered the workers to pile up the bodies of dead Indians for burning. Before the fire started, I had seen and smelled the sores on their bodies.

One night, our masters loaded some of us horses with gold and tied clothes over all of our hooves. They hoped to sneak out of the city on the Tacuba causeway, but the Aztecs had already destroyed all eight of the bridges that spanned its water gaps.

Our men threw the bridge they had built over the first one and we crossed safely. An Aztec woman saw us, screamed, and the Aztec warriors attacked us from their canoes. Our men got their bridge over the second gap and most of us got across before it fell into the water.

Led by Cortez, some of the horseman spurred ahead and Cortez made us swim across the remaining gaps. Behind me, I saw other horses trying to jump them and falling into the water. We reached shore with all of the horses who carried gold on their backs.

Cortez whirled me around and led a rearguard action to help the survivors escape. By then, I could see that the gaps had been filled with the bodies of our men, servants, Indian allies, luggage, and horses.

Those few of us who survived were battered, bloody, and exhausted. Our retreat continued until we reached the Plains of Otompan. We stallions know we might have to fight to defend our herd and all the members of our expedition had become like a herd to me.

In that battle, my master used my sharp bit and his roweled spurs to excite weary me. Blood soon dripped from my mouth and flanks. An arrow sliced across my tender nose and more blood ran from it. A rock hit my master's head and another arrow went through his hand. He dismounted and I got away from him.

My injuries drove me mad and I attacked the Indian warriors with my teeth and shod hooves. As I charged back and forth, I struck them with my front feet and lashed out with my back feet. l also used my teeth to crush their bones and throw them through the air. Those I didn't kill ran away from me.

Ever since men had dropped me into the hold of that ship, I had felt angry and resentful. When I went berserk, I released all those emotions into violet action. Exhaustion finally stopped me and I felt much better, but didn't like the smell of the blood that covered most of my body.

While men cleaned me up, they praised me. Over and over, I heard the same words. "Morzillo, you saved the day. Morzillo, you won the battle for us."

After that battle, we stopped our retreat, turned around, and marched back to the city. Now that I understood my role in battle, I let myself enjoy attacking our enemies. We retook Tenochtitlan and destroyed it.

For five long years, I continued to serve Captain Cortez. Sometimes men brought mares in heat to me and I enjoyed breeding them; but, despite my protests, they never let me court them or stay with them. I dreamed about escaping to freedom with them and some of my foals, but my master kept me too well guarded.

For a long time, I had known that he valued me only for what I could do for him. When he decided to visit Honduras, he chose to ride me. By that time, I no longer felt like a young horse.

He brought his woman with us and she rode beside us. Instead of paying attention to me, he concentrated on her. I still wanted at least one mare of my own. If he could have a female, I felt he should also let me have one.

We marched along narrow jungle trails and crossed many rivers. Everyday I felt more exhausted. Whenever we came to an extra-wide river, the men had to build boats to carry us across. Under my hooves, they shifted about and I hated traveling in them.

One day, we came out of the jungle onto a beautiful grassy area around a lake with an island city. Tame deer grazed there and our masters raced us after them. Whooping with joy, they killed deer after deer. We horses dragged their carcasses over to the campfires so they could be skinned, cooked, and eaten.

The rulers of the local tribe crept out to meet us. They called themselves, the Peten-Itzas, and their city, Tayasal. They asked my master to dinner. He rode me and took twenty men with us.

Before we reached the city, I stepped into a hole and felt an agonizing pain in my left front hoof. When Cortez dismounted, he pulled a large splinter out it and blood poured after it. It hurt so much that I had to hobble along on three legs.

That night, my master left me in the city. In the morning, my groom brought me some grain. As I ate it, he laughed. "We impressed them natives good when we killed their deer. They're gonna keep you, take care of you, and call you, Tziminchac. That's the name of their god of thunder and lighting."

I couldn't believe my master would leave me behind. As he led all of his men away, I whinnied and whinnied, but he ignored my cries for help. I tried to hobble after them, but the natives caught me and locked me into one of their courtyards.

They bowed to me, put garlands of flowers around my neck, and knelt in front of me. They brought me many special meals made out of chicken; but I'm a horse, not a god, and can't eat human food.

Since they didn't know how to treat my hoof, it soon got infected. Soon, I had to give up my dream of escaping to freedom, but hoped that some of my sons and daughters would get away from men. One night in a dream, I saw many herds of wild horses roaming over the plains in the New World.

Without other horses or men who understood me, I felt so alone. As I slowly starved to death, I waited for someone to come back to care for me or rescue me, but my treacherous master had abandoned me.

Soon I saw artists studying me and building a statute of me. The more solid it became, the more life faded away from me. I spent many hours dreaming about galloping over Cuban pastures or watching some of my descendants break away to freedom. Even if the Peten-Itzas continued to worship me, I knew my true legacy was in the foals who would live after me.

Information Sources:

Beatie, Russell H. Saddles. Norman, University of Oklahoma Press, 1981.

Bennett, Deb. Conquerors: The Roots of New World Horsemanship. Solvang, CA., Amigo Publications, 1998.

The Broken Spears: The Aztec Account of the Conquest of Mexico. Editor: Miguel Leon-Portilla. English Translator: Lysander Kemp. Expanded and updated edition. Boston, Beaker Press, 1992.

Cortez, Hernando. Letters from Mexico. NY, Grossman Publishers, 1991.

Denhardt, Robert. The Horse of the Americas. Tulsa, University of Oklahoma Press, 1949.

Denhardt, Robert. "Horse Lore of the Conquest".

Dobie, Frank. Mustangs and Cow horses, Texas Folklore Society, 1940. Pages 197-226.

Diaz del Castillo, Bernal. The Discovery and Conquest of Mexico. Cambridge, MA, DaCapo Press, 2003.

Graham, R. B. Cunninghame. The Horses of the Conquest. Tulsa, University of Oklahoma Press, 1930.

Innes, Hammond. The Conquistadors. NY, Alfred A. Knopf, 1969.

Loch, Sylvia. The Royal Horse of Europe. London, J. A. Allen, 1986.

Marrin, Albert. Aztecs and Spaniards: Cortes and the Conquest of Mexico. N.Y., Athenaeum, 1986.

Prescott, William H. History of the Conquest of Mexico. N. Y., Modern Library, 1936.

Acknowledgements:

Drawing of Conquistador is courtesy of Candace Liddy. Cartoons are taken from the written records maintained by the Aztecs during the Conquest.

Originally Published in Art Horse Magazine, issue 11, 2010, pp. 61-64 and revised for this book.

Author Information:

For sixty-sixty years, Janice Ladendorf has been working with horses. Unlike most amateurs, she has trained her own hunters and dressage horses. One of her interests is the history of equitation and how its principles have been applied through the centuries in various equestrian disciplines.

The University of Minnesota awarded her a B.A. magna cum laude with a major in history and a M.A. in library science. Her further studies have focused on communication theories and animal behavior. They have helped her understand equine behavior, especially as relates to communication between humans and horses.

In her books and numerous articles, she has advocated using humane training methods to build a partnership with your horse. Currently she has three other books and a DVD in print.

A Marvelous Mustang is a nonfictional memoir told from the viewpoint of her Spanish Mustang. As a supplement to this memoir, she has recently produced a DVD from her video records.

Quest for the Silver Mustang is historical fiction. Set in 1832, it is the story of a girl's search for the horse of her dreams.

Human Views and Equine Behavior explains how new scientific ideas can be used to explain equine behavior and the interaction between humans and horses. All these ideas and the related training techniques have been evaluated as she worked with her own horses and observed others working with their horses.

Since she retired, she has focused on learning more about the history of horsemanship and horse breeds. She has published numerous articles on these topics, some of which have been updated and revised for this book.

She has been a research librarian, an inventory analyst, and an accountant. She lives in St. Paul, Minnesota. For more information about her published work, you may visit her website, www.jladendorf.com.

The horse on the cover and page 95 is Syndicated Copper. He is the standing herd stallion for Windcross Conservancy, in Buffalo Gap, SD. He is a bay dun and epitomizes the spirit of a true Spanish Mustang.

There are multiple associations who register Spanish horses with an American mustang ancestry. The five major ones are listed on the next page.

American Heritage Horse Association (AHHA)
American Indian Horse Registry (AIHR)
Horse of America's Registry (HOA)
Southwest Spanish Mustang Association (SSMA)
Spanish Mustang Registry (SMR)

Horses who still live in the wild are managed by the federal government. Information on the National Wild Horse and Burro Program can be found at www.blm.gov. Horses that are adopted through this program generally have a freeze brand on their necks.

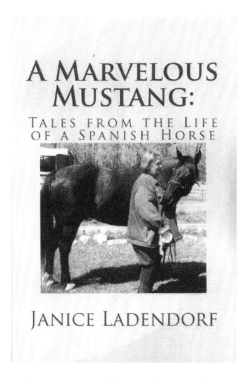

A book for all animal and horse lovers from age eight to eighty.

Paperback $15.95   E-book $5.99
Order from Amazon or any other online retail source.

This fascinating memoir is the true story of the taming, gentling, and training of a wild and fearful colt through his first four years. Step by step, it describes what horses must learn to live safely and comfortably with humans. Written from the horse's point of view, it takes the reader inside the head and into the world of a real Spanish Mustang. As he struggles to accept life among human predators, he lets the reader know how a prey animal thinks about us and what he feels about everything that we do with him.

This DVD is available from Create Space and Amazon for $10.95.

Viewer Comment:

"I was amazed at how readily Skan learned and accepted orders from his human. I noticed she only gave him small steps to learn and built upon that through which he learned to trust and be willing to do what she asked of him. The two of them demonstrated that with patience and persistence a wonderful bond of trust and communication can be achieved between man and animal."

Quest for the Silver Mustang

Janice Ladendorf

Will Lisbet McTavish ever find the horse of her dreams?

Paperback $12.00   E-Book $5.99
Order from Amazon or any other on line retail source.

In 1830, Lisbet McTavish sets out on a perilous quest to fin the silver mustang she has ridden so many times in her medicine dreams. Her hidden heritage links her to the spirit world of our Native Americans. She leaves Virginia and travels by keelboat form Pittsburgh, Pennsylvania to Fort Gibson in Oklahoma. On her long journey she has to deal with thieves, river pirates, men who abuse horses, slave catchers, gamblers and an epidemic. Will she survive to find her silver mustang?

Human Views and
Equine Behavior

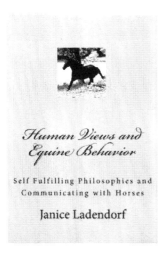

Paderback $15.95   E-Book $6.99
Available from Amazon and other Retailers.

Humans need to see horses as they are, not as they believe or want them to be. An innovative approach to communication reveals new equine abilities and how our beliefs will influence their behavior. These beliefs can be divided into four views about equine nature and management styles. Horses can sense our views and adjust their behavior to fit into our expectations. Regardless of the equestrian discipline, such adjustments will affect many critical training issues.

Human beliefs have greatly hindered our understanding of how we communicate with our horses. When these cues develop into a language of touches, our theories have failed to adequately explain how horses can understand them. This limitation applies to both English and Western riding. Behaviorism provides an excellent explanation of how trick training works, but cannot explain how horses can understand our aids at any location and in any situation. A new answer to this age old puzzle comes out of a detailed analysis of equine cognitive abilities and the language of the aids.

Made in the USA
Charleston, SC
10 September 2015